Tales from Rhapsody Home

Tales from Rhapsody Home

OR WHAT THEY DON'T TELL YOU

ABOUT SENIOR LIVING

by

JOHN GOULD

ISIS
Publishing

Copyright © John Gould

First published by Algonquin Books of Chapel Hill
Post Office Box 2225, Chapel Hill, North Carolina
27515-2225, a division of Workman Publishing,
708 Broadway, New York, New York 10003

Published in Large Print 2001 by ISIS Publishing Ltd,
7 Centremead, Osney Mead, Oxford OX2 0ES, U.K.
by arrangement with Algonquin Books of Chapel Hill.

Library of Congress Cataloging-in-Publication Data
Gould, John, 1908-
    Tales from Rhapsody Home, or, What they don't tell you
    about senior living / John Gould.
        p. cm.
    ISBN 0-7531-6469-8 (lg. print: hc)
    1. Gould, John, 1908-   2. Authors, American – 20th
century – Biography. 3. Maine – Social life and customs.
4. Aged – Maine – Biography. 5. Old aged homes –
Humor. 6. Aging – Humor. 7. Maine – Humor.
8. Large type books. I. Title: Tales from Rhapsody Home.
II. Title: What they don't tell you about senior living.
III. Title.
PS3513.O852 Z4748 2001
818'.5209 – dc21   00-054168
[B]

Printed and bound by TJ International, Padstow, Cornwall, England

For my great-granddaughter
Courtney Gould
with love

April 12, 1997

Contents

Dear Reader:

Tales from Rhapsody Home is this defiant old geezer's effort to help young and not so young folks prepare to become residents in a retirement home. My wife, Dorothy, and I have spent the last four and a half years in just such a place, and I'm happy to pass along some of what we have learned: How to order a jelly omelet after five meals of beef; how to distribute color photos of your spleen operation without making the others jealous; how to play Beano on Tuesday nights and still make Wednesday's group bus to the grocery store. Rhapsody Home is a mythical name, but everything I write is true. Because of the nature of this guidebook, I feel it's best we keep our exact whereabouts unknown.

—John Gould
Somewhere in Maine

In The Beginning

Once upon a long-ago time, I was a fine-looking young man with fire in my eye, zeal in my heart, and a haircut that cost twenty-five cents.

The years passed.

As some can say, I never had a sick day in my life. I spent a good deal of time along the brooks in the contemplative man's recreation, and I did a little shooting, like Venator. I married the perfect woman who mostly fed me things I liked, but other times things that were good for me. Our two youngsters were delivered in Dr. Richardson's front chamber, thirty-five dollars for everything. They grew up without embarrassment to anybody and we are glad and we are pleased. They gave us a full house: queens over kings. The three granddaughters by our daughter, the two grandsons by our boy. All five are good-looking, all are smart, all went through college, all have found work. It seemed to us we had only one thing more to do.

Grow old.

I believe this did not happen all at once, but came gradually over a period of maybe eighty years; and then things sped up.

Edward W. Wheeler, who was counsel for the Maine Central Railroad, moderator for Brunswick Town Meeting, and Grand Master of the Grand Masonic Lodge of Maine, told me once to pay attention to the four signs of advancing age. They are, he said, in this order:

1. You can't remember a name.

2. You can't remember a face.

3. You can't remember to close your pants.

4. You can't remember to open them.

I have not yet experienced any of these. My memory is keen in all respects, and when I had my little shock that began to erode my eyesight, all my friends told me to rejoice that it hadn't affected my able mind and rendered me foolish. I'll leave that for others to debate, but I guess I had begun to totter some, and found a cane useful, at least at times. My wife, Dorothy, still blessed with 20-20, had had a lube job on her hip and got some cleats on a knee, and that slowed her down, so we curtailed our weekly skydiving sessions. And that winter, when I'd gone for my annual flu shot, Dr. David Bradeen had suggested in an offhand way that it might be well for Dorothy and me to consider a place where we could have care if needed. Dr. David was more than just our family quack and I felt disposed to hear him.

Thus the search began for a place to harden our arteries and enjoy the blessings of senility. Dorothy and I left finding shelter to our daughter and her able husband, and they picked the Rhapsody Home we chose. It was an excellent choice, and we moved in just in time to be notified that the rent would increase.

The Window Saga Part I: What I Tell You Three Times Is True

Having made the decision to live in a Rhapsody Home, we moved into this commodious complex, this happy haven for hapless has-beens, this paradise for previously important people, on the fourth day of January 1996. I was eighty-seven and my wife Dorothy was not. We had the blessing of our family, the cheers of some neighbors, the approval of others, and had consulted our postmaster about change of address. We had drained the pipes, terminated our constant bickering with the Central Maine Power Company, and had dealt with a real estate agent about the sale of our lovely little home with fruit trees and a view of the ocean.

This was it. There was no turning back. Henceforth we would be supremely happy in the cozy care of professional cozy career people, those dedicated to loving the old folks and who, in so many artfully chosen words, had promised all our little hearts might desire. Our rent, while steep, was affordable, and it included even a gentleman with the proper tools who would come monthly to shorten our toenails. We never had it so good. Weary from moving, we bade good evening to those who helped us lift and carry, and we retired to our snug bedroom, content.

On the fifth day of January 1996, we entered our first complaint and threw ourselves upon the mercy of the truly fine people who had told us to contact them at once if displeasure irked us in the least. We had slept our first night in the opulence of our new life in a bedroom that could not be ventilated. The only window, I found upon wrenching my back to open it, would not open. It could not be opened. It was not a window made to be opened, but was hung on a slant and fastened to remain so.

Extreme youth was still heavy upon me when I first figured out why we slept in a room with open windows. In Maine you begin to understand a great many things when you are big enough to split firewood. Fresh air was promoted as being good for us, and to insure longevity, the child must learn to endure the rigors of nighttime winter. Chimneys were not built into bedrooms, and the Happy-Times Knit & Sew Club was ever ready to show the young girls how to tack a quilt. I grew up with it and so did my darling wife, whose mother was from New Brunswick. Heating a bedroom was both hard on wood-piles and bad for the lungs. As I recall, my bride wore earmuffs on our wedding night, which was well Down East on a normal October 22. Our hotel room was not heated, but still we opened the window onto the sea to hear the breakers and get a breath.

So I naturally applied myself to the young lady at the reception desk in our new retreat for the elderly, and I said merely that we couldn't open the window in our bedroom.

"Yes," she said. "It can't be opened."

Bear in mind, please, that I was new around here, and had not learned to do without the basic simplicity of previous experiences in the outside world. I was, if you will, a victim of that society that believes in fresh air and ex-pects a bedroom window will be obliging. So the young lady's words seemed askew, and I felt were perpendicular to what I was talking about, so I suppose this led me to some small degree of irritation, which I voiced.

Poised and unruffled, the young lady merely said, "There is nothing to be done about it."

Next, I made the rounds of this illustrious institution, where I had been enjoined to speak at once to anybody about any trifle, and soon decided that "There is nothing that can be done about it" was the standard aphorism to be given to anybody who had a problem. Since my bedroom window had been closed forever when the residence was built, I understood that previous tenants in our apartment had been satisfied with this explanation. I could see that all who gave me this answer were well rehearsed, and they all inflected each word in the same way.

My wife said, "Give up; you can't win!"

My only wife is remarkable, and over the years, I've become attached to her and admire her talents and pay good attention to her precepts. Still I persisted.

I repeated to the management and slaves that custom and tradition, habit and the American Medical Society, every schoolmarm and every P.T. authority insisted on fresh air during slumber. What did they think electric blankets are for? I got the same answer over and over: that's the way the place was built and that's the way it has to be. There's nothing we can do about it.

Do you remember in Lewis Carroll's *The Hunting of the Snark*, "What I tell you three times is true?"

On several occasions I looked up at the window, mostly puzzled as to why that kind of a window should be installed in a bedroom, agreeing with myself that architects must be a silly lot. It didn't take long for an alert, if aged, farm boy to see that there was, indeed, a jolly-good way to do something about that window. It would not be difficult. Unfortunately, I had sold my woodworking tools before we moved; but I was not about to give up yet.

Who Had More Fun?

This business of adjusting, after a scrupulous lifetime of decent living, to the vagaries and double talk of Rhapsody Home, is a matter of degree, of course. About whether man or woman adjusts the sooner, the better, and the more graciously, I have a story.

On sacred Mount Olympus, this story goes, the gods and the goddesses were considering various important matters during their daily preprandial cocktail break, and Father Jupiter offered a subject for discussion. Apparently, as he and the bouncy Juno enjoyed the intimate colloquies of connubial cooperation, they frequently asked each other who was having more fun, he the pusher or she the pushee?

This was the very question he now put to the gods and goddesses at cocktail hour. Were sexual relations more fun for the woman or the man? It was clearly a question without an answer. My wife and I, in our red-hot days, had wondered about that, and discussed it between heats. As close as we ever came to an answer, I said if she liked it better than I, then it was too good for her. We left it in that unsettled situation, and I think we never brought the matter up again.

But the gods and the goddesses are immortal and they had a way to find out! Jupiter merely waved his hand to gain attention, and snapped his fingers. And there before all stood a young man, eager, dependable, vigorous, handsome, fully developed, and incredibly desirable. The gods and goddesses burst into wild applause at Jupiter's creation.

So this young man was set down off Mount Olympus to seek and find a young lady with whom he might dally and so forth. In that vicinity, it wasn't difficult to find cooperation, and later in the afternoon the young man returned to lofty Mount Olympus to say he had enjoyed an interesting experience, and what next?

Then Jupiter snapped his fingers again, and this paragon of manhood was instantly changed into the most voluptuous female ever to grace the countryside. Every vestige of masculinity was erased. But, and this is the important part, this newly made young lady retained all the memories of the previous encounter, and while she was now a female, she knew what it was like to be otherwise. Now she was set down from Mount Olympus and was soon in the arms of some lucky young Grecian chap who happened by, and he fol-de-roled with her in the usual way with abandon and delight, an exercise that took some time but was quickly over, and the young lady was ready to be taken before the gods and goddesses to report.

So you see, there on Mount Olympus, stood the only person ever to experience sex from both points of view. When Jupiter said, "All right, let's hear it," the joint immortal attention was tremendous. For the first time, and to date the only time, this question was answered by somebody who knew. So who had more fun, the boy or the girl?

It's much the same when you ask who adjusts better at Rhapsody Home: the lady or the gentleman? The answer on Olympus was the female, nine to one. Here at Rhapsody Home the ratio may be larger, for I think I detect some areas in which the men do not jump up and cheer whereas the ladies are more receptive. One difference is the relative degree of affliction as infirmities progress. The elderly maiden lady who confessed to adultery told the priest she enjoyed talking about it, and I find (I think) that a good many ladies like conversations about absorbing liquids, liver scans, visual oddities, swollen ankles, bypasses, and shortness of breath. I do not. Except to notice the nurse has nice ones and to wish I was eighty again, I can have my blood pressure read without feeling I must tell everybody. But I notice at supper time the men seem always to be looking in the mashed potatoes for lumps while the ladies gossip about who went to the hospital today and when Mrs. Cranston will have her next biopsy. Of course, we all have our share of problems, but it seems to me that men's lives have not been adorned in the same conversational way and we could use a bit more to talk about.

There is, I honestly believe, some illusory charm about an ailment that beguiles the ladies into fond chatter. They sit pleasantly and discuss their spleens and livers and gastric conundrums, and have a lot of fun, and it may not be altogether frivolous. It may tell us why the women get over Rhapsody Home blahs sooner than the menfolk. Perhaps we'd do better to talk about peeing more frequently and drinking more cranberry juice. Are you aware that having a cataract removed includes a television tape of the surgery? I've been thinking of selling tickets and holding a semi-nar. Let's talk about it and adjust!

Full Circle

The serious lad who prepares when he is young to live in a Rhapsody Home when he is old will want to give much thought to the expected oddities he didn't expect. I was completely unready in this area and damn nigh broke my neck because nobody warned me. When we arrived, we were ready to believe all the nice things Rhapsody Home had to say for itself in the come-on brochure. We were delighted to find ourselves in the relaxed atmosphere of advertised peace and quiet. Cark and care were behind us. Then I fell arse over tin dipper into the bathtub.

Comically enough, my wife had just said to me, "Oh, look! Here's a string we pull if we need help in an emergency!" And so there was! From a place in the wall a string hung down, and day or night, fair weather or foul, we could jerk the string and a nurse would appear in two minutes. We were safe and snug in our new home and had nothing to fear.

And unsuspecting, I went hellity-bang into the bathtub to demonstrate what does happen when the irresistible force meets the immovable object.

My wife said, "What was that?"

I said, "Pull the little string!"

The nurse, who responded immediately, was experienced and adroit. From my smooth profanity she ascertained at once that I was more angered than hurt, and applied soothing words rather than ointment and Medicare forms, and she wanted to know how I happened to fall into the bathtub.

I had been wondering about that.

But I told her that in our family it had long been our custom to climb up on the bureau, disrobe there, and then dive into the tub with two inches of water.

She said, "You could get hurt!"

I said, "I just did."

"I don't find anything wrong," she said.

I said, modestly revealing some of my excessive culture, "There is no opodeldoc for the deep hurt that moans within."

The nurse said, "Garbled, but from *Othello*."

I said I was lucky to be alive to confirm her information.

The cause of my precipitous arrival in the

bathtub was easily isolated. Since Rhapsody Home was built, the linoleum in our bathroom had received a weekly application of a solution applied by the cleaning woman, a preparation approved by the management to promote long wear and tear. This had the effect, also, of making the floor sticky and well ready for me, or somebody else, or 50,000 miles, whichever came first. I, of course, did not go into the bathroom to fall into the bathtub. I was there, business in hand, to make water. I had approached the receptacle in the usual manner, facing forward and without unseemly flourishes. Falling into the tub was the last thing I came there to do.

Having arrived for the purpose aforementioned, I made final preparations, and satisfied myself that I was pointed in the right direction, and to assure my balance I proposed to move my right foot an inch or so to the right. But when I found the sticky linoleum refused to release my slipper, I forthwith hurtled, ballocks, backside, and buff-ahoy, into the tub, which was situated hospitably, and I thumped in a manner that made the pigeons fly in alarm from the Methodist church steeple five hundred yards up the road. I was still going at it pretty good when the nurse arrived.

Supposing I planned to sue, the Rhapsody Home management made every effort to dissuade me, and promised to take care of the gluey floor at once. The report of the nurse was made available to Housekeeping. Housekeeping spoke to Planning. Planning spoke to Executive Operations, and Executive Operations sent a fax to God. God called a meeting of the General Programming Council, and it got back to God on the following Tuesday with a positive consensus. God's quintuplicate order to commence to begin to start to consider, and to originate a pilot program, arrived in a few days and was finalized two Fridays later. The next week a man came with a measuring tape to measure our bathroom, and he said he would come back soon and put down some new linoleum.

Then winter set in.

In my total ignorance of the way to operate a Rhapsody Home, I had supposed that somebody would go to Wal-Mart and buy a pint of that stuff to remove sticky wax, and I would shortly be able to piss in my own flush without starting a Mexican Revolution. But I soon saw that things aren't done that way when you own a Rhapsody Home and have an obligation to the old folks. I was new around here and didn't know much.

Late that summer, a crew came early in the morning, took up our sticky linoleum, and laid a whole new piece before dark. The cement stunk loudly, and we thought about a motel, but by midnight the air was cleared and we went to bed.

So that took care of our first unexpected expectancy at Rhapsody Home, and we had a fine new floor at both bother and expense. We had to be grateful for this special attention.

The next morning the house-cleaning girl came by to tidy our apartment, and she put the same old detergent to the new linoleum.

We're holding our own.

Without Theo

Theo didn't use sticky detergent. Theo had been our *Putzfrau*. One day a week, she would breeze in to razzle-dazzle our small house. She'd change the beds, do the laundry, pick up, and make herself useful. At noon she would sit beside me at table for lunch, salt my sandwich, sugar my tea, and giggle at my small jests. Theo was family. She was an island girl, fetched up out on Maine's only-one "Munhiggin," and she knew how to do things and how to see things to do. We loved her and she loved us, and we were well-enough acquainted so I always promised her a goose on Christmas. She never came to get it, and told people she wouldn't dast go within a mile of my house on that holiday.

I first became aware of Theo when I heard she was the "correspondent" in our town for the weekly newspaper, and forwarded the gossip about who had the mumps, who went to Bangor, and when the new culvert was put on the East Shore road. Some time later I got to know Theo well enough so I asked her how much the newspaper paid her for her faithful work. "Oh, they don't pay me anything," she said. But then she added, "They do give me a free subscription."

A little while later I heard the paper had increased its yearly subscription price by fifty cents, and I congratulated Theo on a raise in pay. And a little after that she told me she didn't write the weekly news from our town any more. "I got other things to do," she said.

As Theo did all the things at our house that Rhapsody Home was going to do for us, you might say we didn't need to bring Theo. Of course we had paid Theo. But now we pay hi-di-ho rent to Rhapsody Home and my wife does the laundry. She feeds quarters into the washer and the dryer, and she brings her own bottle of soap. Then she sorts and folds and puts things away.

Putzfrau is German for charwoman, and I suppose grammatically that's what Theo was. Socially, however, she was a kind friend who used us right and came to do housework my wife and I were no longer able to do. A couple of times during the years that Theo ran our household, visitors from away wondered just who she was, anyway. They thought she must be a relative, as she joined in the conversation, poured the tea, and called us Dot and John.

I think it was chicken livers one day. Theo had said she loved chicken livers but hadn't seen any in years. So we chanced on some chicken livers and bought about a quart of the things to take back for Theo. On the day she came to clean that week, she was all jazzed up at the thought of a whole noonin' with all the chicken livers she could eat. My wife and I, so it happened, would have ham sandwiches, and the precious chicken livers were all for Theo.

And then about half-past eleven a station wagon whirled into our dooryard, and out came Laura Foley, her husband Sam, and another couple that lived next to them in Binghamton, New York. We knew the Foleys from years back, and they and their friends were in Maine for a vacation. And lunch is ready, will you join us?

So they joined us and we all had ham sandwiches while Theo sat and gorged herself on a magnificent feed of expensive chicken livers, done to perfection just the way she liked them. Theo smacked her lips and giggled and kept saying, "They feed well here, don't you think?" As our guests were offered only lowly sandwiches, they seemed quite amazed that our cleaning woman ate so lavishly while we (and they) dined on the economy plan. But of course, Theo was much more than a cleaning woman.

When we moved into Rhapsody Home, without Theo, the windows of our apartment needed a washing they had been denied since the building had been put up. We expressed a desire to see out, and repeated it every few days for over a full year. Let us say we were paying for clean glass and didn't get any. And we lived with the constant realization that Theo would have cleaned our windows without being asked. It took Rhapsody Home one year, four months, and thirteen days to wash our apartment windows, and then for some unknown reason they only did half of them. We were out of the apartment for most of the day, and when we returned late that afternoon our telephone rang. We were asked if our window washing was satisfactory. The voice said they wanted to ask before they put the machine away.

I have no idea what kind of a machine they have, but I betcha Theo is far better looking!

One to Nine

Let's put it this way: I want to be honest about this adjusting business, and I've been thinking some more about how the men adjust and how the women adjust. In truth, we're both just making out and sometimes we adjust to it and sometimes we put up with it. And if, as I have relayed, women have the advantages of intimate conversation, there *are* a few occasions in which the men tend to do better.

I've been pondering on these regular sessions Rhapsody Home has where the residents can come and make suggestions to staff members for, as we used to emphasize at Grange Meetings, the good of the order. First thing to notice is that the staff is so composed that anybody we may wish to see is not available. When Housekeeping is due for a lambasting, Rhapsody Home makes sure nobody from the housekeeping department will be there. The gentleman of the species figures out at once that the gripe meeting is fixed, that it does no earthly good to attend and squawk, and that nobody plans to make any changes anyway. The staff members are on the payroll, you see, and things go nicely for them, and waves are splashy, and what would a rent-paying old fogey know about anything? If I've understated the matter, Rhapsody Home inmates may be questioned accordingly. Such infidelity to our benefactors certainly needs further explanation, and I volunteer as follows.

At one of these grouse meetings, duly called to order in the comfortable library of the institution, where the jigsaw puzzles are done, a group of the high-spender ladies decided to offer a suggestion. We men, naturally, had long since decided there was no point in attending, unless for kicks, so this was strictly a distaff matter and we wished them luck. As I was not present, I can offer only second-hand reports about the matter.

My wife, who was spokesman at the meeting, told me what went on. "How did you make out?" I asked.

She said, "What do you mean?"

I said, "Well, what are they going to do?"

"Nothing. Did you expect they'd do something?"

I said that hope springs eternal in the human breast. It seems the ladies, instead of brushing off the outward prospects that prevail, felt something needed to be done about "organizing" the dining room. This was not really about food, because all of us, boys and girls together, have given up on the food. Slap, slap, and take it or leave it. Instead, this was a suggestion about how the dining room could be set up so we communicants could eat without frustration and without tremendous clamor. The waitresses, for instance. These are young ladies recruited from high-school dropouts of respectable local families, and appraising them in general leads to the conclusion that not a one of 'em knows it is gauche to blow on the cold soup to warm it. They get no training as they start to wait-on, and it seems none has had any at-home background to teach the niceties of gracious dining.

We all loved the little girl who slid the soup in front of us as if launching a bowling ball and cried out, "Here we go!" It was a stirring start on a star-crossed supper and was amusing if not genteel. "You'll spill my soup that way!" I remonstrated one evening, and she said, "It's not hot." It seldom is.

At the meeting, my wife had said, "We think it would be helpful if Rhapsody Home sent one waitress back to the reformatory and replaced her with an older woman who would train the waitresses and explain to them that each table should have butter, cream or facsimile thereof, mustard with bean-weenies, cider vinegar with sauerkraut, and things like that." It's true that night after night we have no butter, the bread is always cold under a foolish napkin, and we do often get apple-sauce spilled on our potatoes.

I asked my wife if she had really thought these suggestions would wreak any massive improvement. "There was nobody there from the Kitchen side," she said, and I told her this aspect of the gripe and grouse meetings had long since deterred my attendance. "Well," she said, "What else can we do?"

I don't often speak to my wife with forked tongue, as it tends to make her surly, and several times to get even she has starched my undershorts, but I thought this "What else can we do?" merited an intelligent reply.

I said, "You learn to like applesauce on the potatoes." But this didn't help. She still goes to the meetings while I stay in the apartment and read something by Euripides by the streaming sunlight pouring dimly through our dirty windows. So I guess male and female adjustment runs at least one to nine.

One further note: Of course, we all have our pet causes and I still persist with my bedroom window crusade. And though I have given up on the complaint meetings, I have other methods up my sleeve.

The Perfect Tomato

Now, please, take tomatoes. When you make the great decision to forsake the ugly old world of fact to take your happy place among the honorable retired, take with you, as I did, all you know about tomatoes. Unlikely as that sounds, believe me. Did you ever know anybody who has two degrees as doctors of philosophy? Without tomatoes you would not.

So I was sitting here in the blissful joy of my retirement home, and I picked up a newspaper, in which I read an Associated Press dispatch that sounded very like what it was—namely, a poop story sent to the Associated Press by a public relations expert employed to do so by a large corporation that has something to sell. In this instance, tomatoes. It seems that at a cost of over five million smackeroos, Van den Bergh Foods, one of the world's largest processors of tomatoes, had just dedicated its Tomato Technology Center at East Stockton, California. The company is seeking, the story said, the Perfect Tomato.

I, myself, have known everything there is to know about the Perfect Tomato for the past seventy-five delicious years, and here I was hidden away in a haven unable to get to East Stockton soon enough to halt this awesome waste of good money. The tomato research center, it said, would be staffed by twenty-eight scholars who would devote full time to the Perfect Tomato search. All of them were educated to the hilt, except some who were more so, and one of them, as I have mentioned, actually held two degrees—a double Doctor of Philosophy. I never heard of such a thing! Why would a gentleman already basking in the brilliance of a Ph.D. spend the time and energy required to get another one? And for gracious sake, why, after he has two of the things, would he want to embrace the curious distinction of being an expert on tomatoes? No one even needs to have one Ph.D. to get in touch with me, and I stand ready at all hours to tell this company all there is to know about the Perfect Tomato. One little telephone call, just like that, and I could save Van den Bergh five million dollars.

I began my study of tomatoes in 1914, the year I was six. My parents had bought a small house at 28 Grant Avenue in suburban Medford, Massachusetts, where we would live for four years, or until I was ten and my father achieved his desire to return to his native Maine. The Medford house was on a double lot, so Dad would have a garden, and come the next spring he and I began to dig and delve. I was underfoot, but I began to learn, and one afternoon he and I walked up Grant Avenue to the greenhouse of Mr. Crockford and bought a flat of tomato plants. One dozen plants, twenty-five cents. We put them in the ground of our vacant lot, and I was accorded full instruction, every word of which I can hear today in my memory.

My father said, "No, don't stand 'em up straight. Everybody stands 'em up straight and they should lay 'em down. Bury the stem right up to the top, and in two days the stem will sprout roots the whole length. You gain a week to the first red tomato!"

So I learned to lay a tomato plant lengthways. First Lesson.

When my father's garden lot began to look peaked for want of nourishment, he showed me where the tomato leaves were turning yellow. Manure we did not then have. It would be several years until, back in Maine, we had our black Jersey, Blackie, to help fertilize. So Dad went to the garden store to see what he could do about pepping up his soil.

"I'd like some nitrate of soda," he told the clerk.

That summer the Big War (now WWI) was hard upon us. Dad didn't know, nor did I, that nitrate of soda was a chemical critical to munitions, and with war going on was temporarily out of supply as a fertilizer for tomato plants. The clerk swallowed, and told Dad, "Well, it's available, and I suppose I could get some. There's a lot of red tape to it, and it's terribly expensive. I think the quote this morning was forty-eight thousand dollars a ton."

My dad said, "Then don't bother. I only wanted half a ton."

In that neighborhood of Medford—Glenwood—lived a number of Belgians, many of them tobacco rollers in the J. A. Cigar factory in Boston. Most all of them kept rabbits, or hares, for Sunday dinners, and most of them had dovecotes to house the pigeons they raced as a heavy-gambling sport. My father made the rounds and cadged pigeon and rabbit dung, and, lacking good cow manure, he used that in his garden. Like a physician in his vigil with a patient, he watched our dozen tomato plants turn green again and set fruit.

After that, until I opted to live in detached senior simplicity, I was not without tomatoes. You don't need a Ph.D. twice. It does help to have a cow. Blackie, our first cow after we got settled in Maine when I was ten, had a cream-line halfway up the pail, but my grandfather, my father, and I in turn knew that her duty didn't end there. Cow manure is money in the bank. Blackie lingered through school with me and became an able Latin scholar. I'd strum Blackie and repeat the conjugations, and Blackie would chew and listen, and while she never went for a Ph.D., she knew the passive periphrastic as well as I did. She never shirked; Blackie never nurtured a poor tomato.

The newspaper story told me the talent arrayed by Van den Bergh, world renowned producer of tomato sauce, included molecular biologists, hybridization specialists (plant breeders), chemical engineers, and assorted agronomy analysts. And I had had a black heifer who knew everything they do!

The day my father and I walked to buy tomato plants from Mr. Crockford, we had a choice of only a few kinds. None was hybrid. One was Erliana, which came early but was inclined to have crooked fruit. There was the John Baer. There was another, usually available then, called Bonny Best, but it was about like the John Baer. The Ponderosa, or beefsteak, was a bigger fruit, but pinkie rather than red, and the yellow variety was said to be less acid and better for some stomachs. That was about it for varieties until one year the Valiant appeared in the seed catalogs, and it was to remain the last and the best of tomatoes until everything went Burpee hybrid. There came a spring when seedsmen no longer offered real tomatoes, just hybrids, and I had to save my own Valiant seeds every summer for next year's garden.

Here in my desk drawer, in this paradise for Old Seed Stock, I have some Valiant tomato seeds in a little envelope, ready to sow in a flowerpot next spring. The Valiant is the Perfect Tomato. I could have told that to Van den Bergh Foods, which grows hundreds of mixed-up varieties every year, but is still looking for the best.

The Perfect Tomato is not the one you measure in millions of tons or set up huge research laboratories to study. It is a single tomato, clinging to a vine in Maine until it is really red and the sun has done its best. And the perfect one is not just a random happening. You need to grow it yourself and you don't need a college degree. You will of course need to know how to milk a cow.

Here's what you do: After you have "sot" out your row, or field, of Valiant tomato plants, you stand back and look things over, and you play around in your mind with the dewy morning in July when you will eat, all by yourself, alone, the first ripe tomato of the year.

You lay down your hoe and walk to the stone wall around your Down East field, and you find one rock that is a bit more than bag-pudding size, and you tote it over and lay it beside one of the tomato plants you have just planted. It doesn't matter which one. My grandfather taught this to my dad, and my dad taught me, and now my son thinks about it in turn, but he lacks Valiants and lives in another day and another world and so on and so forth.

My grandfather was a great one for bucolic surmises, and he computed that a rock laid by the roots of a tomato plant would be a fine asset in a dry summer. He never tried to fetch a rock for each plant, but he began bringing one rock to do duty by one plant, and that was the plant that grew him the Perfect Tomato each year. When that plant set its first tomato, and June was well busted-out all over, Grandfather would give the matter daily attention and begin to yearn. Now he would bring a saltshaker from the house (something he taught Dad and me), and he would put it under a flowerpot so it wouldn't get wet, and he would bide.

The day, when it arrived, was always the day before tomorrow. Tomorrow, he would eat his first tomato. In my time, Grandfather was old and lived alone, and I was too busy being a youngster to be with him on that day. But this is how he described it to me. After barn chores and breakfast, he would put on his haymaker's straw hat and walk up to his crops. It was the time of year when the bobolinks shout when you come into their fields, and he took his time to admire his friends. Coming to his tomato patch, he would uncover his saltshaker and make sure it would run free when he shook it. Then, ceremoniously, he would tip his first luscious Valiant so it broke away at the stem, and he would give it the same evaluating scrutiny a Tiffany might give the Hope Diamond. And he would say, "And God saw that it was good." He'd rub the little darling on his shirt, not so much to polish it as to assert his approval. Then he would take a bite, and then he would salt it, and then he would stand there in the morning sun, the hillside dew-pearled, and he would eat the whole thing and lap his fingers.

He had found the Perfect Tomato again!

And I did the same thing, over and over again, and now I'm doing it once more in my recollection. Except, of course, I'm on a salt-free diet and it's the wrong time of year. Never mind! The Van den Bergh company will never find the Perfect Tomato in California; it's here in memory with me, to brighten my days in this Home of Rhapsody.

More about Dirty Windows and the View at Rhapsody Home

A lifelong Vermonter returned from his first visit to Boston and was asked what he thought of the place. He said he guessed it was all right, "but you can't see off." Since there are a great many places in Vermont where that's all you can do, I know what the old fellow meant, and I must add in my own dialect that Rhapsody Home is much the same. Even if our windows were not dirty, as you have heard, we cannot sit in our fine apartment and look off over brave horizons to perilous seas and faery lands forlorn. Rhapsody Home is not on a hill, and the highlights of our regular view come in two short moments daily, save Saturday and Sunday.

The first is in the afternoon as automobile commuters return from their city business to the waiting suburbs. A red light stops the traffic automatically so the people in the vehicles can pause and think what cussed fools these mortals be. I never lived that way, and if I had, I'd have damn-well found another way to get home. The second of the two moments is in midforenoon, when the youngsters attending the day-care school are released for exercise and we can watch the eager little boys chasing the hopeful little girls in a fruitless game we have named "just wait a few years." There are swings and scooters and climbing rigs, and even a big tractor tire to climb on. The ages are such that no little girl has been caught yet.

The slide intrigues me. At, I'm sure, great expense, Rhapsody Home management, which operates the preschool activity as well as the other advertised services, has provided an aluminum slide, which is not enough to threaten mayhem to the ages involved, and which the kiddos mount by walk-up steps. From the platform aloft the young-uns must arrange themselves as if to slide down the chute, but they don't go anywhere. The incline is insufficient, and things at rest tend to remain at rest. Another two degrees of grade might make the difference, but the slide was designed, we can see, by a numb cluck instead of a physicist, and Rhapsody Home got swindled when it bought the thing. I suppose, too, the kids got swindled when they got enrolled by their parents. And the parents who pay got swindled as well.

Usually this recurring tableau has one kid perched on the point of no-go and all the others poised in some posture of patient possibility, and nothing happens until the bell rings and a teacher has to come and push the kid. The descent is not speedy. Mostly, a child will go halfway down in modest hesitation and then hump his backside along to the bottom. It is, however, fun to sit at my window and watch one of the teachers manipulate that *geller hintern* around and about in her effort to get the brat sliding. All the scenery is not in Vermont.

All little girls are pretty, and I sit here at my apartment window and feel sorry for the poor little boys who can't catch one. The traffic and the playground have their daily times, and then the window of Rhapsody Home has nothing much to offer. As a window, it is in the wrong place by many long miles. Boston, even, is better.

But one day, when we hadn't been here too long yet, I noticed, as I sat looking off, a neat bungalow. We didn't know who lived there. When we liquidated and came to Rhapsody Home, we had no means to visit around and get acquainted with the natives. We've lived rather much within our group of fellow has-beens. Now this bungalow became a window amusement and we kept an eye on it. Every morning there was a hefty laundry on the line, and we wondered if they took in washings. At times, we saw a little girl, and she seemed to have a puppy.

We noticed one day that they were putting up a beautiful Walpole fence. This interested us because the Walpole pale that they put up costs a bundle at the Walpole mill in the Maine town of Detroit, and anybody with a Walpole fence must be prosperous. The Walpole Woodcrafters are based in Walpole, Massachusetts, and you'd suppose that when they built their mill in Maine they'd have built it in Walpole, Maine, not Detroit, Maine. But they didn't, and the thing to see in Walpole, Maine, is not a sawmill but a beautiful colonial meeting house kept in mint condition where all are welcome. In the summer the pulpit is supplied by volunteer reverends from elsewhere who are willing to exchange a few words for a week's vacation by the sea.

One summer we heard the Reverend Willard Heimbech of Leavenworth, Kansas, would come. As he was known to us, our son asked him to christen his firstborn in the historic Walpole meetinghouse, which was done so successfully that Grandson William has never had to have it done again.

So clearly you can see that a Walpole fence meant something to us as we looked off through our dirty Rhapsody Home windows, and we were glad to find our unknown neighbors were so well-heeled. But the fence obscured the wash line and then the little girl, and we had nothing to watch. We had the daily traffic and playground moments, but since our windows gave us nothing much else to see, even darkly, we were lonely and bereft, with Christmas coming up. Then, four days before Christmas, we saw that the Walpole fence was hung with Christmas lights, and behind it a growing spruce was aglow to its beautiful tip. Joy to the world, peace on earth, and come all ye faithful! During the evening we agreed that this was so nice that we should telephone our unknown neighbor to say thanks.

My wife said, "Who are they? We don't know who to call!"

Our Rhapsody Home management, when asked, said there was no problem, that the people next door were named Grant and they lived on White Birch Lane. We found six columns of Grants in the phone book but none that lived on White Birch Lane. Then I wrote a note and asked somebody's delivery boy to leave it at the red bungalow across the road. It was the afternoon that would ripen into Christmas Eve. All at once my telephone jumped about in a glad paean of holiday cheer and I answered with my usual friendly enthusiasm.

I said, "Not on your life! I'm not about to pay you one red cent! The kumquats were squishy, and we had to throw them all away!"

A pleasant female voice then said, "Oh, I guess I have a wrong number!"

I said, "Not at all, this is Santa, and have you been a good girl?"

In this way I became acquainted with our neighbor. She said she'd got my note and nothing had ever pleased her more. She was delighted that she had contributed to our Christmas. I asked for her name and address, and she said it was Profenno and they lived on Red Oak Lane. I said that was close enough.

She said it was close enough so she was looking up and could see in my window.

I expected her to remark that my window was filthy, but she did not. Then I remembered. It was Christmas Eve. Thanks to Mrs. Profenno and her holiday lights, the Rhapsody Home windows were shining tonight with a different brilliance.

Activities

All our lives until now we have done some things for duty, some for prestige, some for fun, and a few for the hell of it. But now we are happy residents of our joyful Rhapsody Home and Old Age has decreed that we must give our attention to Activities. Activities are what you do to kill time now that you are on the shelf and would otherwise have nothing to do except go for groceries on Wednesdays, which is an Activity you do not do on other days. The poet Wordsworth somewhere mentions somebody so bereft for something distracting that even a stuffed owl was enough to cheat the time. At places like Rhapsody Home, everybody willy-nilly gets a stuffed owl.

I was six when my father said, "Trout bite best when apple orchards bloom." He took me to Purington's Brook and introduced me to my first trout. Since then I have been a devout disciple of Isaak Walton, although it would be some years later that I read *The Compleat An-*

gler and comprehended "the Contemplative Man's Recreation." Long before I knew about contemplation, I knew that a walk along a brook and the concomitant meditation would be balm to any life-size disturbance. My dad also taught me to leave my fishing pole where it would be handy at all times, preferably by a back door so I could sneak away unnoticed. I thus had an adequate and satisfying answer to ennui any time I could work up some ennui. Not that I was really a shirker, but I was never one to hang around while folks thought up things for me to do. But here at Rhapsody Home I don't get to go fishing, and this irks me not only in general, but in particular now that the years have added up and I can have a complimentary fishing license from the state. I can only wonder if Purington's Brook would still have a trout.

No, I'm not bad-talking a happy subject. Activities are good things. In season we have bus rides to see the spring flowers, the apple orchard in bloom, the fall foliage, and the Christmas lights. Also Halloween goblins. Yes, we did those things before we came to live at Rhapsody Home, but now they are included in our rent and have become Activities. They are management's kindness, regimented opportunities to keep us from climbing up the wall with the blahs. Our stuffed owl.

Activities run from basketry to slide lectures about health among the Peruvian Indians. It doesn't take much to interest nonactivists in a sedentary retirement home whose alternative amusement is listening to hearts palpitate. The Professional Activities Expert who arranges these golden occasions is aware of this and avoids quality as much as possible, which is a lot. We recently had a concert of ancient Scottish music on a Spanish guitar and a tin horn. Everybody came, expecting a piper. It is possible, I am told, for an advanced and deft piper to play "My Old Kentucky Home" on a doodlesack, a dexterity the Scots call *dooblin'*, but to a late moment no honest musician has attempted "The Bonnets of Bonny Dundee" on a Spanish guitar, except at Rhapsody Home. It was bad, and several critics followed me out.

When the ombudsman comes to see how we old duffers are making out, they show him the list of scheduled activities, and he goes away assured things are fine and the management is just wonderful to us. It was such with the magician who never showed up. We all pay for our Activities. We pay too much, because we pay well for so many things we don't get. A short time after we moved in, one of the things we paid for and didn't get was a magician. I never did any magic myself but in my home workshop I've worked out some gadgets used by some manipulators, and if I don't perform, at least I know how a trick is done. I like to watch a good illusionist do his stuff. So I descended to the Activities room early to be sure of a front seat. My confreres and concubines gathered and sat in orderly fashion and waited and waited and so forth and so on. No one came. We never heard what happened, and we didn't see the Activities Director.

As we dispersed, an experienced resident confided, "No use to say anything, they know what happened. They do this on purpose."

"How so?"

"Well, there's no magician. If there's no magician, they don't have to pay one, but the record shows they had a magician. You must be new around here."

The first thing to learn at a retirement community is how to find amusement in the dreadful. The magician who didn't come turned me toward poetry. I didn't suppose that I was a poet. But I've come to write many a merry jingle about Rhapsody Home calamities that amuse my fellow tenants even more than the calamities do. Poetry is good discipline for prose. It makes one careful with words and familiar with their shades of meaning. It teaches that a word must sound right as well as be right.

The first of many Rhapsody Home jingles was about the absent magician. It was pinned to the bulletin board at 5:24 P.M. and management had removed it by 5:26 P.M. It ran thusly:

Presto!
The great magician passed us by;
We have no notion where he's at.
We came to see him mystify,
And pull his rabbit from his hat!
What black magic have we here
That makes magicians disappear?
'Til he returns we'll have
To wait to see him prestidigitate.

The management said I had offended the staff. Hosswhiffle!

Let me not be unkind. My life before Rhapsody Home was not uneventful, but as a journalist, and something of a good one, I was more of a spectator than a participant in the work and play of mankind. There was a jaded detachment from the profanum volgus and its adoration of human foibles. I had to be neutral. But now there is a schedule, and when it's time to do this, I do this. I try to join in the Activities with respect. When it's time to say the carrots on my plate are not cooked, if that's an Activity, I comply. Even when we don't have carrots.

So regulate your preparations as the years sneak by, and be ready, when it's your time to go to Rhapsody Home, to embrace the Activities.

Dr. Plummer

As I have advised in an earlier chapter, when you choose a Rhapsody Home and go there to live out your time, get one where you can look off. But even if there is nothing much to see, you can make do, as I do, with the reruns. Take with you to your Rhapsody Home all the memories you can muster of good times and good people, and have them ready to oblige when opportunity calls. They will help adorn your twilight vistas. Right now I'm remembering my friend Dr. A. W. Plummer.

Doc was still practicing in his nineties, and as the state would no longer issue him a driver's license, he had to make arrangements for somebody to drive him on house calls. I had offered to do so, and for a few of his last years I'd arrive to find him ready to go, his black bag at his feet. This was in the Maine town of Lisbon, where he practiced.

Just once did I apply to Doc as a patient, and he took two dollars from me as he did from all others who came for medical attention. I did, indeed, have a bug in my ear. I was keeping a cow, and when I walked up to the pasture one evening to bring her down to the barn for the night, a foolish little moth of some sort appeared out of the dusk and went into my right ear. I saw the thing coming and knew what it was. Then began a series of frantic efforts by the moth to get out of my ear and fly off on his business. These efforts came about every ten seconds, and, while they were unsuccessful, they set up an incredible racket for me. I got the cow down to her stanchion and went to find Dr. Plummer. By the time I got to his office, in his home, I was a mess. This thing sounded like a bombing aircraft flying over, and while I was getting no pain I was slowly going wacky. I burst into the Plummer surgery and yelled, "Flush the bug out-a my ear!"

Doc said, "Which ear?"

Doc was a logical positivist.

I said, "The one that's got a bug in it!" Then the moth let go again and I climbed onto the top of Doc's bookcase.

A squirt of warm water from a syringe did the trick, and I looked at Doc as he examined the wee beastie in a small kidney pan. He said, "One of the *Hymenoptera*, and we'll send it to the Smithsonian. I tell you, John, I had a patient back years ago that caught a *Hymenoptera* in his ear, and we didn't get it, and it brought off a hatch of maggots."

Doc was tall, spindly without being at all skinny, and had a goatee that was the only one of its kind in town. His medical education had been interrupted by a bout with what was then termed consumption, but he licked it in a sanitarium in New York State, mostly by his rigid submission to rigid discipline. That the Doc lived to be ninety-nine affirms recovery. Dr. Plummer was the total answer to the French definition of a gentleman: *Le vrai honnête homme est celui qui ne se pique de rien.* (A true gentleman prides himself on nothing.) No specialist, he, but rounded in every direction. Doc was a student of human affairs. Medicine was but one of his directions, even if his trade.

The doctor's interests had no boundaries. He knew his Bible and all the great authors well. I never found a topic he couldn't embellish. At public suppers, church, and lodge, I'd contrive to sit beside Doc, and as he tucked his napkin under his collar he'd say, "Well, John, what shall we discuss this evening?"

One evening I said, "How about the atomic swerve of *De Rerum Natura?*"

Doc said, "You want to take pro or con?"

* * *

Doc, whose deeper sympathies were everlastingly Republican, posed as an uncompromising Democrat, and he did serve one term in the state legislature. He loved to ride over to Augusta to testify before legislative hearings, and his opinions were respected. I drove him to such hearings many times. I remember one in particular. I forget now what the bill was about, but Doc felt it ought to pass, and he told me all about it as we rode to Augusta. He was most eager to speak in favor of the bill. When the hearing began, the proponents of the bill arose in turn, urged passage for this reason and that, and then the chairman of the committee said, "Dr. Plummer, do you wish to speak now?"

Doc unlimbered his long legs and stood. I can repeat his remarks precisely today. He said, "Thank you, Mr. Chairman. A. W. Plummer, M.D., Lisbon. Mr. Chairman and Members of the Committee. I came to this hearing prepared to speak in favor of this bill. But I have listened to the remarks of the supporters of the bill, and I have changed my mind. May I postpone my remarks and speak later as an opponent?"

When Doc was into his nineties, he was clambering around on the shore rocks at Orr Island, and he fell and broke a leg. His left leg, since you ask. It was a long carry from the tide to the ambulance, and a long ride to the Central Maine General Hospital in Lewiston, where he was honorary staff. The next morning, hearing about this, I hustled to the hospital, where I found Doc in the front tower room, finest in the house, a nurse attending his every need, and a pair of crutches leaning against the headboard of his bed. A sumptuous collation was before him.

"Come in, come in!" he called. "Here, Nurse, can you find John a beaker of orange juice?"

He told me falling to break a leg was foolish and he hadn't meant to, but he'd been reading about periwinkles earlier, and that day he was picking up different kinds to look at them. Somehow, in the excitement of getting him on a stretcher, his can of winkles had been lost. As soon as they discharged him, he was planning to go right back out to Orr Island to search the rocks, he said.

Dr. Plummer never got to live in any kind of a Rhapsody Home. Widowed, he lived alone a number of years, but had women come in to clean. On random evenings I'd stop by to sit a spell, and I always found him in his lounger with a book.

The word ran about town one morning that old Doc Plummer was losing his swifties.

One of the Wonnerbergers was coming home late, and, as he passed, he saw Doc Plummer in a nightgown out with a flashlight walking around in his garden and talking to himself. And it was so, because other people, going by, reported the same thing. The old sawbones was crazy as a coot! Everybody was sad.

When I heard this I went in to see Doc. He was washing his noontime sandwich plate, and I set down the piece of apple pie I'd brought. "What gives with you and midnight strolls in the pumpkin patch?" I asked.

Doc said, "How'd you know about that? I've been adjusting my new sundial. I always wanted a sundial, and I found a good one at Minot in a junk shop."

Doc said there's a lot goes with setting up a sundial. The thing has to be synchronized with the sun, and then there's an angle with the polar star. He'd done a lot of reading about sundials. Nothing modern about them. The ancients had them. Accurate if they're set right. He thought he had his just right. But he had trouble with his logarithms. He hadn't worked with logarithms for a good many years, and he'd lost the knack. Besides, it was hard to read the logarithm tables with a flashlight, and his eyes weren't tip-top now. I told quite a few people that they didn't need to worry about Doc Plummer's losing his marbles. He never did.

* * *

When Doc had a house call up toward the town of Webster, he'd stop on his way home and sit for a time in a rocking chair at our kitchen window. It was a gentle rocker, and came to be known as the Dr. Plummer Chair of Applied Wisdom. The windowsill, right by his elbow as he lectured, had two brass plaques I'd stolen from railway windows in Europe: *nicht rauchen* (No Smoking) and *défense de cracher sur les tapis* (Forbidden to spit on the carpets). He'd sometimes have a cup of coffee. If my wife went about the housework and drifted away when some abstruse conclusion was about to evolve, Doc would shout, "Dorothy! Come here! I want you to hear this!" Dorothy always hurried to give ear.

Doc read everything and never forgot anything he read. In his first year of practice he had a baby case at Webster Corner, and he arrived much too soon. Instead of returning to town and making a second trip more on target, he decided to wait things out. He found a rocking chair and a couple of pillows, and he looked about for something to read. He said, "That house had only two books. One was the Bible, and as I knew that fairly well, I took the other one and sat down. It was a book of knitting instructions."

If you're not familiar with knitting instructions, they run largely to P for purl and *K* for knit, and the rest is numbers telling how many stitches to purl and how many to knit. Dr. Plummer learned to knit while the baby was deciding to appear, and all his life he made his own mittens and his own socks.

When Doc was ninety-nine, he felt some old, so he went up to spend the night in the hospital. He was in the same tower room as when he broke his leg a few years before. His nurse made him ready for the night. Then he said, "I think, Nurse, that you've done just about everything for me that you can do."

"Yes," she said, "just about. Now, have a good rest! Good night."

Dr. A. W. Plummer said good night. And he didn't wake up.

The Window Saga
Part II: Fan Notes

As has been reported with stifled yawns, our first problem with management after we happily matriculated at Rhapsody Home was about our bedroom that we couldn't ventilate. My favorite wife and I had suffered for over sixty years in bedrooms that reeked of cool, bracing, invigorating, health-bearing, northeast wind off Canada's expansive Gaspé Bay, and every precept we had heard about proper habits told us fresh air while we slept was not to be questioned. I reiterate what management told us: There was nothing that could be done about it.

I continued to complain vigorously, and during the next months, among the things management tried to do about this serious matter about which nothing could be done was to supply an electric fan of great surge and passion. The fan's purpose was to take air from a window to the westward in our living room and move it by Queensberry Rules through a doorway into our bedroom where it would keep us healthy while we slumbered. This was not unlike sleeping on the afterdeck of a ketch during a line storm, but we hoped we might grow accustomed to it and wake each new morning fit and fierce.

Truthfully, this did not happen. We did not get used to it, and we found management had left no forwarding address. To make a long story comical, we slept on our ketch from one February to the next, and until the twentieth of the second March. On the twentieth of the second March the fan squawked at the bearings, coughed, choked, strangled, and took its own life in a gurgle of despair.

There were some side effects to this fan, like the epileptic seizure warnings described on pill bottles. One of them deserves description so people in Rhapsody Homes can avoid similar situations.

The fan was so positioned that anybody going to or coming from the bathroom, for whatever reason, was obliged to walk with a sharp lookout through a gale of wind. Anybody with a cane, walker, or wheelchair, either singly or in convoy, was wise to whistle and so on, and proceed at peril. And at approximately this time I developed, but not on purpose, a swelling at my ankle, which caused our good house physician to pull at his chin and say h-m-m-m. He concluded I was having an internal problem with liquids, and prescribed peeing pills, one every other morning and two on alternate mornings. This gave me some-thing to do, and also fixed me up for dinner conversations and daily progress reports. I now had something to bat back over the net when Mrs. Cummings told of her back and Mr. Gurnheit of his gas. But there was a price: I had to spend much of my time fighting that damned fan for a crack at the receptacle. Be-cause of the poor air conditions in our bed-room, we got so we didn't turn the fan on and off, but left it running. Our apartment had two directions: upwind and downwind. The television was to loo'ard and the microwave to windward. Every ten minutes I'd pass to re-lieve myself, praise the Lord and curse the management.

I now digress. Years ago up in that part of Maine known as Tuttle-Brown country we had a talented gentleman in the town of Wellington, pronounced Wellin'tin, who in-vented an entirely new kind of windmill. The standard windmill, such as in Holland, must be pointed into the wind if it is to work effi-ciently. The Dutch windmill is accordingly built on a turntable, and as the wind shifts the table turns and the wind is always right. Our gifted gentleman in Wellin'tin took care of this until everybody was saying, "Why didn't I think of that!"

Instead of a horizontal shaft for his wind blades, he fitted the blades to a vertical shaft, so everything turned in the manner of a merry-go-round rather than a pinwheel. The blades were thoughtfully cupped so they drew wind in one direction and spilled wind in the other, thus allowing for constant operation so long as the wind blew. He put his mill in a square tower, with open places to receive the wind.

Now, that part of Maine has never been seriously considered as a nursery for brains, and the appearance of this mill astounded one and all. This windmill that appeared was true genius, and people came from all around to see. And sure enough, whichever way the wind chose, the mill noticed no difference. Then one morning this gentleman took an oil can, and because it was just about sunrise and the wind was quiet, he stepped between two of the motionless blades to lubricate the main bearings. This he did but, while he was inside, a breeze sprang up, the mill began to turn, and he couldn't get out.

Now people really began to come to see the windmill, and after some ten days, thousands of people were standing around. They could look through the whirling blades and see the inventor inside, fuzzy as it were, and they would wave at him and he would wave back. The weather forecasts called for continued wind, and bets were placed that the inventor would not survive. But he did, and immediately devised an escape hatch.

I have digressed in order to say that we have lived somewhat similarly imprisoned by a windmill. But we do get air in our bedroom, which proves you can do something about that which nothing can be done.

The demise of our electric fan was dramatic. The very sound told us the ailment was terminal. There the thing stood, four feet tall on its tripod and post, silent at last after its warranty period. We notified Maintenance, requesting the courtesy of a work order, and suggesting we could now try again to fix the window.

Response was immediate. We cannot complain in any way. Rhapsody Home takes care of its own. A tap at the door, and in came a maintenance man with a new fan.

And we're back where we started.

And I was told, long ago, that the Wellin'tin vertical windmill, up in Tuttle-Brown country, has an escape hatch that can be opened only from the outside.

Cooking School

My wife was an only child, and her devout mother kept her framed wedding certificate over her connubial bed to prove copulation was sanctified. My wife's father was an upright, respected, honest Christian, although a Baptist, and the framed wedding certificate perhaps explains why my wife is an only child. When I evaded the chaste convent of my wife's maidenly girlhood, she would often quote Sunday School memory gems while I had other things on my mind, but I was early struck with her willingness to adjust.

My wife's mother and my own mother were natives of Canada's Maritime Provinces, well-brought-up young ladies in home-cooking households. In both kitchens the objective was to prepare unlikely materials so they were nourishing and palatable to hungry folk. My mother taught her two daughters all about cooking, but I, being a boy, was not meant to become a wife and cook, and didn't get the pantry training. Still, I learned some all the same, even if it was about tricks instead of ingredients. Well, I learned not to lift the cover on the stew pot while the dumplings were cooking—unless you want a stew of wallpaper paste. I learned to scramble eggs on a slow fire and stir them until done. At an early age I could singe a hen with a burning page from the newspaper. (My mother insisted the brisk editorials in the *Lewiston Evening Journal* singed a hen better than the senseless rantings of the *Portland Press Herald*.) She showed me how to poach a weenie so it didn't bust a gut and blow apart and look indecent, and she told me always to put an onion in the pot of baked beans. As you may have ascertained by now, the food here at Rhapsody Home is not always up to the lower end of institutional standards. I have told the management of Rhapsody Home that I am ready and willing to help at no charge. My wife is willing and able as well, and she knows a thing or two about how to teach cooking.

In their age, and after our own children were grown, my wife's parents came to live with us. In those days the elderly were not sidetracked into Rhapsody Homes. When her father died, my Dorothy was grieved and bereft, and she chanced to see in the paper that students were wanted for a Federal gravy-train project. It was a cooking school, except that it had a high-sounding, pump-priming name thought up by Eleanor Roosevelt. Funds were there to lift the underprivileged into dignity and prosperity, and nobody in the depressed common crowd seemed interested. Unless students turned up, the thirty-million dollar grant would have to be withdrawn. My wife said, "Why not? It'll give me something to put in my time!"

So I called a friend at the state house, and he said, "Why not?" and she was enrolled.

I had noticed she was moping some about her dad, and I hoped this would be a good distraction. She would not only have professional instruction, but it would cost nothing, and Uncle Sam would pay her so much a day to attend! Shortly, they'd scoured up enough "eligible" students and the cooking school opened. We had had a good fall of snow on the night before, so I had some work to do before she could set off to class. I had to get the tractor out, plow the driveway, and sand the little knoll by our RFD box. Then I got out the family Model A and warmed it up. I had supposed that, at a cooking school, the eager scholars would cook their lunches, but no, she was taking a cream cheese and olive, and a tea bag. Also, an apron and a pot holder, and I stood by as she drove off. Then I went in the house to find she had made my breakfast before going to cooking school, and I had oatmeal, hot cream-tartar biscuits, homemade strawberry jam, pancakes and maple syrup, a pork chop, mashed turnip and home-fry potatoes, perked coffee and a doughnut, and a note that said: "Apple pie on pantry windowsill."

While I dawdled in my lonely gluttony over these cakes and dainties, my wife drove the eighteen miles to the school and found the other students ready and waiting, all eager for the cook-down. The instructor, a professional cook engaged at great taxpayers' expense and not accustomed to Maine winters, never arrived, supposing that because of the snowstorm there would be no school. Sizing things up, my wife said, "No need of wasting the day, everybody find a place, and I'll teach!"

And that's what she did.

As you can see my wife learned quite a lot that she already knew at cooking school. And as I have said, we have both offered our kitchen services more than once to the powers that be at Rhapsody Home. But each time we get the same sensible answer—the management is perfectly happy with the food.

Grievances Regarding Dining

Now seems an appropriate time to discuss dining in a little more detail. This chapter must be read with great discretion, for much of it is about esoterics and things that could be misunderstood if you are not careful. It's like my wife said. She said, "You want to tell about the good things, too; not just the bad!"

I said, "Both of the good things?"

And she said, "What was the other one?"

The food here at Rhapsody Home is as good as anywhere. Everything is of the finest quality. Then they cook it. But in fairness to the kitchen, if you don't care for any of the dinners offered, they will gladly make you a jelly omelet. This they do well, and it is as delicious as any omelet you ever had anywhere else. One evening, after five consecutive suppers featuring beef, everybody had omelets.

One of my ambitions is to compile a cookbook on institutional food, telling how to take good things to eat and render them bad enough to serve at Rhapsody Home. It's the little things that rankle—the way the food's prepared and the way it's served. Below are my reflections on some courtesies that belong with gracious dining that have not been included in our experience here. I include this list at the risk of sounding like a grumpy old man. Skip this one if you don't want to see me look bad. If you do read on, afterward you surely will say, yes, but all these annoyances can be found in restaurants, too. But Rhapsody Home is not a restaurant. It is my home.

So here goes.

The mint jelly is aimed at but never hits the roast lamb, and the raisin sauce is slapped close by but never reaches the baked ham. The cold bread is kept cold in its dainty basket by a linen napkin, but the bread is from an apprentice baker, so it doesn't matter. As to the relish dish, it seems so simple in its purpose and pleasure, why don't we have one? A pickle or two, any style, radishes, cucumber, celery, maybe scallions.

At Rhapsody Home a cup of tea is made with a tea bag and warm water. It is served in the heavy crockery pot before it has drawn and without concern for how one wishes its strength. The mug provided was meant for coffee, which doesn't mind. Tea minds. And why must I peel my sugar? They knew about sugar bowls in the Middle Ages. I get two little packages of sugar with my tea, and I have to drop everything while I tear open my package and turn out what little sugar is inside.

I've given up about substitute salt. More than a few of us lovable nonagenarians have been told to lay off salt. Rhapsody Home, although repeatedly asked to get some Adolph, will not. I bring my own shaker and leave it on the table. Usually the waitress picks it up to put away in the cupboard, gives the cap a sturdy turn so I can't get into it again, and then forgets to set it out the next day. The ground black pepper in our table shakers is too coarse to pass through the small holes in the caps, so we bring our own pepper as well. It's the little things.

Sharing our dinner table, a charming matron sits at my left, and she always starts her supper exercises with a cup of hot water. Blest if I know what she does with it, but we two inspect the cup every evening before the waitress decants the water, to see if the cup is clean. At least five evenings a week, the cup is not clean, and the lady asks the waitress to bring one that is. This the waitress does with a patience to match that of the lady.

The "surprises" are more troubling yet. Recently we had a run of mashed potatoes that were too thick for wallpaper paste and too thin for priming a canoe. After a couple of months, this proved tedious and we gourmands were glad to find a hot German potato salad on the dinner menu, which is posted in the mornings. We liked the idea, and we lolled around all afternoon in hope and desire. A special hanker held sway as we appeared that evening in anticipation. A merrier gathering never gathered. But when the doors opened, we found that the treat we'd awaited all afternoon had been crossed out with a lead pencil, and, instead, we would have mashed potatoes. No explanation, no apology. This did prompt another of my jingles, which, as always, was promptly removed.

Surprise!

Management's so good to us
We really have no cause to fuss
Each afternoon they think about
Supper things to do without
The menus tell us what they've got
And delete whatever they do not.
It's jolly fun to take a chair
And dine on food that isn't there.

My indignation becomes most savage, however, at the prandial speed imposed upon us by the unkind exigencies of the Rhapsody

Home decorum. Our evening refection is brought to an abrupt end with a furious flurry of finality with much banging and slamming by the waitresses, who can't be kept beyond the hour. The waitress brings my plate and wants to take it before I've put the butter to my cold bun. She doesn't ask if I've finished; she can see if she looks but she doesn't look. Why must good people who have dined a lifetime in leisurely pleasure retire to a Rhapsody Home where the waitress must hurry home to see the latest TV show?

One young lady did snitch my plate, and I told her if she tried that again, I'd hit her with my crutch. But the last word was hers: she said, "We gotta get out-a here!"

Indeed.

Wise Old Bongo

It had been another beautiful day at Caucomo-gommoc Dam, and after baby sleep all night, Bill and I awoke to the lilting cry of the festive moose, singing in exultation that all was still right with the world. The orient sun had gilded the sky in all directions, and Bill and I knew we would have another boundlessly beautiful day. Let me explain.

Bill's daughter married my son, and when they told us that they would marry, Bill and I thought we should get to know one another, and this led to annual visitations to the North Maine woods, where we enjoyed the comforts of a camp otherwise kept for workmen sent to care for the dam at the outlet of Caucomo-gommoc Lake. For nearly three decades we did this together every July, observing Bastille Day and doing other exercises, if necessary. It was on the twenty-eighth visitation, as I recall, that the lovely morning described above dawned for us, and from that date I have observed my senility.

So on that lovely morning I stepped from the camp at Cauc Lake, and I turned to greet Bongo, the wise old gull of Cauc Lake, who has been sitting where he sits for about 150 years. He sits on a boom pier. This is a cobbed pier made of logs and stone that holds a boom in place. A *boom* is a string of long logs that direct floating logs in the lake toward the sluiceway in the dam. Logs have not been sluiced here in many a year, but the Great Northern Paper Company employs the traditional wise old gull of Cauc Lake to keep an eye on things, and the gull is pleased to work at such a handsome salary when all he has to do is watch me and Bill every morning for one week in July.

But on this occasion, the wise old gull seemed a bit fuzzy, and he looked to me as if he might stumble into the lake any minute. "Bongo has the jitters," I called to Bill.

Bill said, "He looks all right to me!"

But he did not look all right to me, and I assumed that during the night I had sustained some impairment to my vision that had also hit Bongo at about the same time. I called to Bill to say, "I've lost some eyesight!"

We broke camp the next day, on schedule, and I was able to drive home, but it was our last retreat into the wild Maine woods, and the last word on Bongo. The eye doc told me he'd fix me up in good time. The following winter, at the recommendation of our doctors and our children, we moved to Rhapsody Home. That would be 1996, and Dorothy and I would be married for sixty-four canty years.

I suppose my first inkling that I was wearing out my physical assets came some years before the incident at Cauc Lake, with the discovery I had a hernia—what earlier generations called a breach. Dr. Will Spear assured me after we exchanged jokes that I did, indeed, have a good one, and that it was, as I told him, on my left side, which is closest to the heart. I told him I had acquired this during the mountain climbing when I was doing a picture story for the National Geographic Society magazine on the Islands. Of Langerhans. Will said he'd always wanted to go there.

Will said he hadn't been doing much except now and then to take off a wart, but he would reserve me a place with Dr. Clapp, who was competent and needed the money. Dr. Waldo Clapp, which was his correct name. Dr. Clapp made the needed repairs, and told me he couldn't have done better if he'd had three chances.

Some time later, I began to pee with reluctance, and as Dr. Will had ceased to practice, I went to see Dr. Henry O. White, whom we called Hank. Hank introduced me to Dr. Nuesser, and I had my second surgical operation. It, too, was successful, and since then I pee with vigor and considerable confidence. But I don't go camping at Cauc Lake anymore.

The Indian name *Caucomogommoc* is supposed to mean place-of-the-wise-old-gull, and I don't know if Bongo, the wise old gull that sits forever on a boom pier at Cauc Lake, is waiting for Bill and me to return or if he's guessed what's happened. Bill and I regularly wondered if Bongo was not the same old gull who sat there when Cauc Lake was named. If, over the years, a Bongo has gone his way now and then and been replaced, it was done quietly and without public notice. All gulls look alike, as do all boom piers.

Just to his left, as Bongo sits there in pensive pose, there is the Siss, an inlet to Cauc Lake coming from Round Pond. It's a few miles of quiet thoroughfare, and there is but a slight current, as Round and Cauc are about the same altitude. Moose in numbers haunt The Siss, chewing lily pads. The water is warm, and perch abound in The Siss, so right at hand Bongo has his food. He can load up on sustaining fish and be back on his boom pier in minutes. Bill and I watched Bongo leave for lunch many times. He needed no takeoff room. A foot above the lake, he'd glide right into The Siss and out of our sight without a single pump of his wings. Sometimes there would be a moose, or some moose, feeding where we could see them, and Bongo would just soar over them with a few inches to spare, and they wouldn't look up. Then Bill and I would see Bongo come out of The Siss and resume his sitting on the boom pier. We never saw Bongo perched on any other boom piers in Cauc Lake. Maybe it doesn't take much to be a wise old gull.

I don't know where Bongo passed his winters. He could go a few air miles and subsist on a town dump, or he might take the Atlantic flyway and disport in the luxury of the Bahamas. Cauc Lake, by Thanksgiving, would be frozen over, and free perch would not be readily found. Perhaps, Bongo just moves down to salt water and finds a harbor pile somewhere to sit on until ice-out.

As for me, I am now living in a house of good repute, enjoying the comforts and attention due me, another derelict washed up on the beach of social benevolence. I just hope that Bongo, the wise old gull, is not in the same predicament I am.

The Good Things, Too

A gentleman whose wit and wisdom please me, and who is kind enough to stop now and then to share my time, was recently minded to reprove me on the matter of jocularity. He was wound up and full of his subject. My friend seems to think my attitude toward this institutional life in our asylum is unduly undignified and I should mend it forthwith. He may be right. He says nothing is all bad, and I should try to change my negative point of view.

This is not, he says, a home for hapless has-beens, as I so humorously dub it, but is rather a repository for memorable experiences, where ancient mariners gather after lifetime voyages and offer their experiences for the public good. Here we may listen to the voices of the past, the raconteurs of all ages, places, and topics. Here is everything worth hearing, spoken by somebody who was there. Here the aphorisms of immemorial time are waiting to be considered, and here the present judges the past to admonish the future. Here we have all we want and need.

There was more, and I became convinced he was tutoring me to good purpose, for I felt I had missed the point in my adjustment to my new situation in this lovely paradise for privileged hunters home from the hills and battle-scarred old codgers sitting around listening to their hearts palpitate. I shall not, I told myself sincerely, treat my lot in other than respectful mood, and I must refrain from making small jests where solemn attention is due.

I had thanked my friend for his sage comments, and quickly reminded myself of all the things Rhapsody Home does well. I offer some of them here and cannot wait to see my friend show appreciation that I have listened!

It is true that in the event of need, all services are ready. The house physician is able and has a firm handshake to inspire confidence. I like him because he laughs at my jokes. He is always responsive and makes regular calls, floor by floor. Postal service going and coming is at the lobby desk, and there sits a telephone custodian the clock around. Of the several registered nurses kept on duty by Rhapsody Home, one is considered the resident and is always available at the pull of a string. If a lamp bulb fails, it takes no time at all for a boy to arrive with a ladder and a new bulb. There is a bus that transports us to the grocery each week, and makes other group trips to shopping malls and to sales. At times we go by bus to lunch at a restaurant, and I notice everybody has french-fried potatoes, which Rhapsody Home does not serve. Holidays call for parties, and each month a cake is lit for those having birthdays.

When we moved to Rhapsody Home, I had not expected to find a triweekly cocktail hour on the schedule. But if anybody enrolls in a Rhapsody Home thinking he will be off on a merry toot, he wants to cool down at once. Some do lap the stuff up, but mostly the inmates take a cautious approach. A jolt of jolly-water is incompatible with medications and promotes physical instability that serves no purpose beyond cheering up the bone specialists. The social hour, coming just before dinnertime, brings together all the glad news of the day, and gives members a chance to consider the various plights and difficulties. Nobody knows everything, but everybody knows something, and the consensus after joint reports went like this one recent evening.

Anna was rushed to the hospital
Anna had a cramp in her thigh.
Anna was not rushed; she walked

So her thigh was not cramped.
It was not Anna
It was Charles.
Anna is all right
She is in intensive care
She came home for breakfast.
It was Mrs. Dillworthy, Clarice
Clarice had indigestion
It was Mr. Dillworthy, George
George broke his leg.
Anna will stay overnight for tests
Mr. Dillworthy has a stiff neck.

Charles (we now find out) was in banking. Hester taught school. Minerva had a gift shop in Myrtle Beach. Warren was insurance and real estate in Binghamton, and Geneva, who was a legal clerk in Tulsa, had never heard of Binghamton. You name it, and Rhapsody Home has somebody from there, or it doesn't. Amsterdam, Holland, and Phoenix, Arizona. *"Zum Wohl!"* I say, and Emily lifts her glass to clink mine and chirps, *"Dankesehr!"* Once a day we salute at cocktail time, she with her sparkling water and I with my eighty-proof orange juice.

There are also worship services we may attend, with clergymen or deacons coming in. A hairdresser who barbers, too, is available daily. Some special errands call for a fee to Rhapsody Home, and this includes ambulance, available as needed. The Rhapsody Home library is well used, and a book is much tattered, but the town and state libraries will send not only books, but talking books and anything else. Pharmacies will deliver.

All these adjuncts to happy senior living help us through our tedious days and amuse as well as edify us. All such services are cheerful and in folksy good fellowship. A gentleman in the next cellblock to me has a toy fire engine, so one day I took my toy manure spreader and went over to play with him. We did have such a good time! He suffered somewhat from smoke inhalation, but he is all right. Then we started my manure spreader, and we forgot it was in gear, and we made a hell of a mess.

A young lady who is a therapist comes to show me how to lift my leg and count twenty-five, and then lift the other leg. In this way, the ravages of senectudinality are charmed away, and if I keep this up, I can one day skip rope and play duck on the rock with the unfettered youngsters. I persevere, and it should be but a few days now. I lift my atrophic leg and say one, and I lift it again and I say two, and it takes about an hour in all, and then I can put on my mittens and go down in the elevator and frolic in the fresh air. A hapless reliquary has-been, so to speak, but I am not going to put it that way as I consider my posture in the new meanings of my admonishing friend.

Today, as I approach the main entrance lobby and the fresh air, there is a new bounding in my stride, a new exuberance in my heart, a new way to look at things. My friend was absolutely right. I must thank him again. After all, these folks harbored here at Rhapsody Home are good people, all of us. We have all done important work in this world and are having the reward that is ours. We have raised mannerly children, consorted happily with husband or wife to the betterment of the neighborhood, and are no strangers to human nature and the causes of affairs. Lifelong couples come into the dining room hand in hand, feebly perhaps but cheerily, and those who come alone are buoyant of spirit. The gentlemen wear jackets as gentlemen should in a dining room, and both gentlemen and ladies bring pictures of grand-youngsters to show and brag. I think you will not find a more gentle and genteel group.

Back in the lobby, the United Parcel man was just coming in with a bunch of bundles, and he pulled his canvas go-cart to one side so I could step through the door.

"Good morning," he said with a mighty smile of good cheer. "How's everything this morning in God's waiting room?"

Aha! I thought of a saying I once carved over the mirror on a bar. "Nur mit Humor dein Sach bestellt, dann lacht dir froh die ganze Weld." For those unfamiliar with Schiller, or whoever it was, I translate: "Order your Schnapps with a smile, and all the world will rejoice!"

The Two Keiths

It is a duty of all old people to tell old tales. So here is one about my two friends Keith. They shared two things: the name Keith and a love for neat cattle, or oxen. Both of them were down-Maine and called oxen steers.

Elmer Keith was my neighbor and a long-time friend. He was brought up well-informed and able in all directions. Elmer became an expert mechanic and repairman on anything, operated a sawmill, did highway maintenance, farmed, treated sick dogs and cats, and farmed some more. In his time, he owned many a piece of farm machinery, but relied on his steers. Mostly, he raised up a bull calf, contriving to have two to match, and I believe sincerely that Elmer Keith had no peer in the training of animals. Love, never fear, was the emotion he imparted. I've always smiled at the docility of well-trained oxen that, even when turned into the pasture to graze and be free from each other, will move side by side, going about all day as if they were yoked together. When Elmer let his steers out to graze, the first one through the tie-up door would stand and wait until the other came to stand beside. Then they would walk away, shoulder to shoulder.

In late summer and in the fall, Elmer would take his oxen to the fairs and compete in the pulls. Blocks of granite on a stone drag, or a stone boat, were pulled by each competing pair, and the prize and ribbon went to the yoke that covered the greatest distance in a given time. When the oxen stopped, that was it. Elmer's wife, Sally, used to sew Elmer's blue ribbons into throws and put them over the furniture in her sitting room.

It was a joy to watch Elmer in the pulling ring. He had a goad, the mace of the ox-team-ster, but it had no brad. The stick was never used to urge Elmer's steers. He'd have a hand on the horn of the nigh ox, and he'd lean so his mouth was by the animal's ear. Some driv-ers would whoop and shout and prod with the goad and put on a big act. Not Elmer. He'd suck through his tooth, and make compli-cated noises with his lips, and lean his shoul-der into the ox.

Some reformists have deplored ox pulls as cruelty to animals and persisted in demands that they be outlawed. Elmer used to scoff at the very idea. They revel in the exertion asked of them, he said. Now you and I may not be sure about that one way or the other, but when Elmer said it, I respected his understanding of animals. I always thought Elmer might know how his steers felt, and perhaps the do-gooders who nowadays write letters to the editor lack some of his understanding and knowledge. When Elmer sucked through his tooth, the oxen knew what he meant and gladly responded.

Keith Burns, the other Keith, also teamed steers and competed at the fairs, frequently pulling against Elmer Keith, but never coming in better than second place. From the first time they met in the arena and competed heads on, yoke and driver against yoke and driver, Elmer Keith always took home the blue. And the purse.

Keith Burns lived in the town of Union and had a slaughterhouse. For a man who, like Elmer, loved his draft cattle, this was perhaps an unseemly calling, but that's what Keith Burns did. I got acquainted with him by buying some manure for my garden. I heard he would deliver a heaped-up load for a decent price, and it was good stuff. When I telephoned, Keith said he'd come the next morning, which he did. The load of manure he dumped by my small garden was powerfully redolent, and several neighbors, some as far away as East Friendship, said they had wind of the matter.

The manure of Keith Burns was different because of his trade. Farmers would bring animals around in the afternoon to be processed, and the beasts would spend the night in Keith's special stable, emptying their tracts before their slaughter, and their dressing was not mixed with straw, shavings, musty hay, and distractions common otherwise. The manure was hundred percent clear quill, ready to assimilate with my soil and promote agricultural prosperity. I used to boast that I would have to run after I dropped cucumber seeds, or I would get strangled by the growing vines. Folks living ten miles away would say, "I wouldn't wonder." Until he died, still a vigorous young man, Keith Burns brought me his yearly load of slaughterhouse manure, and I was known throughout Knox County for my beautiful garden.

So it came about that I knew Elmer Keith and I knew Keith Burns, but I didn't know they knew each other and competed at ox pulls. And it was at Litchfield Fair that the two Keiths resolved their competition and gave me something to remember with relish and amusement and discernment now that I have so much time to think. They shook hands warmly as good friends, and not as gladiators about to tangle, and Keith Burns said, "I don't know, Elmer, why I bother to pay my entry fee every year and come here to pull when I know beforehand you'll get the blue again. Some year I might just's well smarten up and stay home."

Elmer Keith said, "You'll beat me the first year you learn to think like a steer. Your trouble is you think like Keith Burns."

So it came about. Elmer Keith said, "I'll drive your steers and you drive mine, and I'll take home the blue."

And that's what they did. Each worked the other's yoke about the fairground a few times, and then they went to the pulling ring, each with the other's steers.

Elmer Keith won, hands down. Quite some time later Elmer Keith told me all about it. He said, "You see, Keith Burns didn't know how to communicate with my team, but I knew how to communicate with his. I just sucked through my tooth, and off we went."

Every so often something makes me think of the differences, and I like to dwell on the Keiths. There's a lesson in here somewhere.

And yet, strange things happen. One spring Elmer Keith told me he planned to grow an acre of cucumbers for the pickle factory and he'd like to borrow my walk-and-push seeder. He came and got it, and I told him when the vines were ready to bloom I'd bring over a hive of bees and leave them at the head of the planting. Bees make cucumbers, I said, and I had a strong colony. So in the cool of one evening after supper I ran the hive over to Elmer's. We laid down two planks for a stand, and the next morning I checked and the bees were flying in good shape. I told Elmer it would make quite a few dollars more in his pocket. He didn't know much about bees, so I told him to let the hive alone and I'd pick it up after the bloom. But Elmer Keith, who could sweet-talk a yoke of oxen into a five-hundred dollar purse, took the advice of the pickle people and sprayed his acre of cucumber plants with rotenone to kill all the pesky little cucumber beetles. This also killed all my honeybees.

You see, honeybees have no ears and are deaf as stone posts, so Elmer can't communicate with bees: it does no good to suck through your tooth.

And if you think I got away from my topic, which is Rhapsody Home, you're wrong. For activities tonight, we've got a slide show about oxen.

She Couldn't Pee

Here at Rhapsody Home you will have observed a familiarity among the residents that permits casual conversations about bodily functions. Things that were not considered polite to mention are now respectable topics, and you've got a fine subject and will have an attentive audience if they do a hip job and get a thousand ccs. It so happened that I was aware of this difference before I moved in, but if a sensitive person unaware should suddenly be exposed to such super-adult matter-of-fact details, embarrassment might ensue. Maybe you haven't been told that old folks talk bluntly about such things.

I did know it. When I was a sprout, I used to go and visit my grandfather as often as I could. It was a twenty-mile ride on a cross-country electric trolley-car line, and then a two-mile walk through the woods to his farm. I'd find him somewhere on his hundred acres doing any of the forty-one thousand things done on farms in the good old days. He was always glad to see me and stopped whatever he was doing. My visits would amount to a day or two, no more, and he was always glad to teach and I was glad to learn. I cherish my memories of Grandfather resting after supper and before bedtime as I read to him from his Bible. Cat on his thigh, feet up, he would loll in his easy chair and prompt me when I stumbled on a word.

On one such visit, he told me that tomorrow we would ride up to Webster Corner and see Myrtle Winstead, who had been ailing. I surmised she was Grampie's girlfriend from bygone days. And ride up we did, putting the great bulk of plowhorse Tanty into the sharves of Grampie's famous three-dollar buggy. The buggy had belonged to Julius Woodrow, agent for the cotton mill, and it had been custom-built, it was said, for seven hundred dollars. Grampie bought it at the estate auction for three dollars—rubber tires, patent-leather seat, saucy whip, and all. The whip had a fluff of red ribbon by the stinger, but was ornamental only as far as Gramps was concerned. Tanty walked along the road in his sleep, the same way he cultivated tomatoes, and beating would do nothing for his speed. He did not fit in the thills, and he gave an undignified touch to the buggy, which was really a splendid thing. We arrived in a very long due time at Myrtle's home, and she greeted us at the door. Tanty got the hitching weight and we went in. Grampie carried a comb of honey for Myrtle. He kept bees, and a box of honey was his trademark when he needed a gift.

At that time I didn't realize that I was learning about getting to be old. Myrtle was old. Grampie was old. Tanty was ungodly old. And I was new.

Myrtle accepted the comb of honey and excused herself to go to the kitchen, where she put the honey in a cupboard and then fixed sugar cookies and raspberry shrub for her guests. We sat on chairs waiting, and then she came with a platter. It was my first raspberry shrub and delicious.

"Well Myrt," said my grandfather, "How've you been?"

"Miserable," said Myrt. "Real poorly. How about you, Thomas?"

My grandfather said, "Can't complain. But you're the one's been ailing. What's your trouble?"

It was just plain fact that I didn't know people went into details about such things, and as a polite little boy trained in euphemisms, I didn't expect what I heard sweet old Myrtle say. There she sat, feminine as my own careful mother, pink apron indeed, and with Grandfather Thomas bending toward her she said, "I couldn't pee!"

Grandfather, who was losing his hearing, said, "What-say?"

"I said I couldn't pee!"

Grandfather said, "Oh?"

Myrtle said, "Went the better part of a week 'thout." Grandfather shook his head, seemingly meditating on the matter. Myrtle said, "I got Lennie to send Dr. Potter, and he come and put the tube to me."

Grandfather said, "What-say?"

"Doc Potter dreened me!"

"Doc Potter, you say?"

Myrtle said, "Eyah, got more'n a quart!"

"What-say?"

"I say he got more'n a quart!"

"What-say?"

"I say he got more'n a quart!"

Grandfather said, "You don't say!"

Myrtle said, "After that I felt some better, and I'm taking pills he left."

In this way, at thirteen years of age, I learned about such things and was being prepared for old age in a retreat for senior living. Here at Rhapsody Home there is rarely an entirely good day, and if at suppertime everybody is at hand, don't forget the day is not yet over and the ambulance is ready to roll. When the victim returns, following treatment and repairs, she will have the undivided attention of one and all. And even if, as I have mentioned already, the women are better conversationalists, the men have a stake in such things, too. When I hear these discussions, I try to smile and think of Grandfather and Myrtle, who shared, that afternoon, their woes and maladies in detail, giving both of them pleasure.

So now, as Mrs. Rancourte passes around the color photographs of the work they did on her spleen, I try to see the beauty in them. Of the dozen shots she showed us, we agreed on one in particular, which she used on her Christmas cards.

Ailments might be awkward, but they make something to talk about. I listen, here at Rhapsody Home, and I try to be sympathetic. It helps to remember dear Myrtle Winstead, Grampie's girlfriend, who couldn't pee.

An Emergency?

When my best critic, and so far my best wife, asked me not to harp so much on the irks, I forthwith obeyed and mentioned our charming nurses. They are great. I, who had a minimum of attention from nurses in my healthy time, became composed about this and accepted the nurses readily as something to be grateful for. This may be a service that comes with the rent, along with the electric stove and housecleaning, but tender, loving care does not truly derive from the price by the pound. A nurse is different, and bless 'em all! Not only that, but now I find that my need for this tender care increases as the days roll along.

It began when Young Doctor Bradeen decided I needed a monthly vitamin shot to maintain my good looks, my humor, and my energy so I could more easily disport with my rubber duck in the bathtub. The nurse, you see, would come at 6:00 a.m. one day each month and needle me from dull lethargy into bouncing buoyancy. I'd get the stuff at the pharmacy and she'd do the rest. My nurse was pleasant, as well as professionally disciplined, and she took about two minutes and was gone.

"Come again!" I would call as she went out the door, and then I returned to bed until the coffee bubbled. One morning this nurse took a blood sample. When she came back to report the results, she told me my blood was thin and that I should be careful not to cut myself or scratch if I itched; bleeding was to be avoided. There could be complications until such time as my circulation was brought to a proper density.

She asked, "Do you use a razor?"

"Only when I shave," I replied.

"That's dangerous. Don't you have an electric shaver?"

I did not. She said to be safe I should use an electric shaver, as the slightest bit of bleeding might cause problems. I do not know how much my new Remington shaver cost, as somebody took care of that errand for me and the bill hasn't come yet. I have used it since it came and still prefer a blade, but I am skittish about bleeding to death. Are you paying attention?

We were at the late-afternoon social hour, and as I lapped down my orange juice, I put my left hand to my left ear and discovered I was bleeding. My wound, whatever caused it, was at the top of my ear, and blood was flowing rapidly. The words of my dear nurse were remembered, so I quickly took my leave, holding my bandanna to my streaming ear. Not my usual nurse, but another of equally fine disposition, arrived at our apartment almost immediately. She said I must have scratched inadvertently, and told me the bleeding had stopped. She put on a Band-Aid. I was all right, and she would look in before bedtime to check. I shortly regained composure.

I was, indeed, all right, and when the nurse returned about 10:00 p.m. to check me out, I told her that all the talk about my thin blood had caused me to become anxious when I found I was bleeding.

"Yes," she said, "I had your records and expected to find you worse off. You were smart to call us at once. But everything looks all right now. Good night!"

With my next bill for rent, Rhapsody Home included a fee for the nurse that night. "It was not an emergency," they told me at the desk. Had it been an emergency, no charge.

So folks, be sure and have an understanding of these subtleties before you move into a

Rhapsody Home of your own. If you're going to need a nurse, be sure you know what an emergency is. Don't panic. If you have a seizure, ask first if this is routine or an emergency.

As a wordsmith of recognized standing, I am aware that an *emergency* is a situation that requires immediate action, and I had supposed, with some confidence, that my bleeding to death might not be something we could postpone for a week or so. I smiled magnificently as I pondered how I didn't die and thus blew quite a few smackeroos.

Thank you for patiently reading about my ear; I know this tale began in praise of our splendid nurses, and there is the moral. What nurses do, and the care and the attention they provide, are mighty important. Such kindness is even more important when a Rhapsody Home decides *your* emergency is management's way to make a fast buck. For in the short run, which is the run we have, kindness and peace of mind will prove to be the one comfort that counts. And remember, if you're going to have a heart attack, make it a true emergency and save some money.

Cribbage and Cookies

Activities are big here at Rhapsody Home, but in my humble opinion, our principal lack is really a cribbage game. Cribbage is a great substitute for therapy, for two, three, and four players. We brought a cribbage board to our new residence, and it solaced my wife and me as we struggled with distressful vexations imposed by our unpleasant landlord, the cad. We've been saddened that others living here do not know how cribbage can cheer one up and forestall the grumps. These others seem to us to be good cribbage candidates, likely to play a good game after some instruction.

Cribbage has been the lumber camp game used to assuage the tedium of stormy days and long winters. It was the shipboard game for seamen on yearlong voyages to Australia. It has always been the game in fire stations where the laddies sit waiting for an alarm. Cribbage was played in every railroad smoking coach; the board was waiting and the brakeman had a deck of cards. On a ferryboat, if you notice, the elapsed time shown on the schedule, island to mainland, always allows for three games.

So you see, cribbage is not unimportant. We have many folks here in Rhapsody Home who remain aloof, but would be closer if we had a vigorous cribbage set-to. It promotes the kind of enmity that makes such good friends. There is a German woman here with whom we have never really become chummy. We would like to brush up our not-very-good German with her, but she doesn't seem disposed. One day she said a bee stung her, and since I know something about bees, I felt this offered an opening.

"Did it leave a stinger in your skin?"

"No, why should it do that?"

I didn't know enough German to continue. So I didn't. It goes to show only that cribbage should not be neglected as a valid activity if you don't care, or are unable, to talk about bees.

We had another lady here who stayed a while and then moved, and I suppose cribbage might have kept her. She had had a career with the State Department. She said she'd been in Paris for years, but she had always used the back door of the Embassy and so had never seen the statue of Benjamin

Franklin by the front door. While she was in Paris, Dick Watson was our ambassador to France, and she'd never met him. She might have if she'd played cribbage. Dick was very good at it.

There's a dear lady here who paints and has something on the bulletin board each day to please us. She sits in the refrigerator management calls the library and does her stint. She often has mittens on, so it's great fun to watch her. I tried several times to have a talk with her without getting far.

So you see, most folks are friendly, but there are many who don't bounce back the ball so readily. I keep thinking the icebreaker we need is cribbage, the great friend-maker.

Grammy Benck loved cribbage. Grammy Benck was a neighbor in my boyhood, and she first appeared unbidden in our home the day my baby sister was born. I was ten, and this was a home job, so things were at sixes and sevens at breakfast time while mother made up her mind and the doctor was on his way. My father was making oatmeal porridge and couldn't find the salt.

Grammy Benck was a huge woman and wore men's size sixteen felt lumbering boots around the house. She had the feminine traits of a wheelbarrow, looked a good bit like a

Clydesdale, and had the loving heart of a front-row angel.

She came through the shed into our kitchen that morning without knocking and said, "I seen the bedroom light on during the night and knew I'd be wanted. Here's the salt."

Grammy Benck, who was no Grammy to us at all, then went upstairs to check on Mummy and came down to tell us everything was under control and to ask if we wanted one egg or two. She loved cribbage.

She also made the best molasses cookies in town. I offer the recipe herewith.

Soft Molasses Cookies
Makes 24 three-inch cookies

1 stick of margarine, melted
½ teaspoon ground cloves
1 cup white sugar
½ teaspoon ground ginger
½ cup dark molasses
½ teaspoon ground cinnamon
1 egg
½ teaspoon salt
½ cup milk
¾ teaspoon baking soda
2½ cups all-purpose flour

Start by setting some shortening aside, handy, because in a moment you will be greasing two cookie sheets. Preheat oven to 375 degrees. Grease two cookie sheets with shortening and set aside. Combine melted margarine, sugar, molasses, egg, and milk. Beat well. Sift together flour, cloves, ginger, cinnamon, salt, and baking soda. Add dry mixture to molasses mixture, one-half cup at a time, mixing well after each addition. Drop by tablespoons onto cookie sheets and bake for just ten minutes.

Cool on wire rack, ring my number, and I'll be right over.

And should you think a good recipe for molasses cookies is a crazy thing to find in a book about senior living in a Rhapsody Home, there's only this to say: when your time arrives and you move in to become one of us, you'll probably adjust all right; but you'll find a molasses cookie now and then will help a great deal. Especially if they don't have cribbage.

Insurance Truth

I would not write this unless I knew it to be true.

I always had been kind to my insurance agent. Every check went forward the day I got a bill, and when we met it was a moment of delight. I was covered, and if calamity intruded, I had a friend. Our decision to move into our new home with the old folks was not all that difficult. We liquidated our assets, gained a place, and hurriedly put our little home by the seaside on the market through a friend who is a real estate agent, and we moved out and we moved in. It took only a day's passing. This was a moment of vast confidence. We had done it! Everybody had been kind and thoughtful, and a new serenity settled upon us. We would adjust to this, our new life, in leisure, and happily live out our days pleasantly. Our home was for sale.

Then we heard from the insurance company. They had forgotten all about us, and addressed us as "dear policy holder." The letter said that since our house was vacant, they were terminating our policy.

Nice people, there!

Now, in pure but innocent ignorance, we did a very foolish thing, and we urge all incipient oldsters not to do as we did. We simply assumed that because our agent was such a decent sort we could rely on him, and as we expected he would be in touch right away we did nothing. More than that, we relied on a curious Maine situation that seemed to us a reasonable one. From the Piscataqua River at New Hampshire, easterly for twenty-five hundred miles to the Bay of Fundy, the Maine seacoast is lined with extremely valuable summer residences that are cozily insured at the highest values, and all of them are vacant from Labor Day to Memorial Day. Add to that uncountable inland summer cottages on lakes and streams and hunting camps on precious spots used also for vacations, and you'll find a great part of Maine residential property is vacant most of the time. You'll find, too, that only when you get old and have your sweet arse in a sling does any insurance company write any letters about terminating your policy.

My insurance agent, the one who always rose and shook my hand in warm affection, laughed in my face over the telephone and said the insipid "I'm sorry!" and gleefully chortled,

"There's nothing I can do about it." (It is no coincidence that this is Rhapsody Home's favorite phrase as well.) "Nothing I can do about it" does not mean there is nothing he can do about it, because there are things he can do about it. It means, rather, that he ain't about to lift a finger in your behalf, and all that big hooraw for the past fifty years about friendship and palsy-walsy was just a little playful crap, and farewell sucker!

Like so many unkindnesses that persist in mortal affairs, it isn't always the thing that's done; it is the way it's done that hurts. You can stab your dear friend, but you don't need to twist the knife. A snide insurance agent who spies to find you have moved to a retirement home could very well give you a ring to tell you his company doesn't like empty houses and to suggest you make arrangements. Or, when his company denies you, he could get in touch at once and offer to find another kind of policy, or whatever. Not so, dear chum! He prefers to be an insurance agent. Agent, that is, for the company and not you. Never you, and bear that in mind.

The whole is predicated on the sacred nature of the insurance company under the law. There is no requirement whatever that an insurance company be decent. I wonder if I ever told the story about my blacksmith shop? I didn't? I will.

* * *

When in my eager youth I bought the local weekly newspaper operation, I became owner not only of the publication, but the three-story building in which it was printed. So I went to the L. A. Jack Insurance Agency and requested fire and liability insurance, and received as usual the warm handshake, protestations of deepest love, and the assurances of continued close attention. When I got the bill I paid it, and then I felt the rate on my fire insurance was pretty steep.

It was away-way out of line. Being mesmerized by the agent's great affection for me, I was cautious about this and asked some questions up and down the street until I was well satisfied this sterling friend of an agent, and his company, were top-quality crooks, and I was being abused. Then I spoke to the gentleman.

"I can't do a thing about it," he said. "It's the rating bureau. You're a high risk!"

"What makes me a high risk?"

"The blacksmith shop."

"What blacksmith shop?"

"The one next to you. Blacksmith shops are high risk."

The nearest blacksmith shop to my property was twenty-six miles away in North Greene. I did find by consulting the town records that Jarvis Lane had once operated a smithy next to me, but he died in 1866, and the shop was torn down in 1867. Now it was 1946. It also occurred to me that I had never heard of a blacksmith shop that burned down, or was a fire hazard, or risk. There certainly was no record that blacksmith shops in the aggregate offered evidence enough to warrant total suspicion.

I said to my kindly insurance agent that he was a thief and his company a robber. He said all I had to do was apply for a rerating, and he felt sure this would solve everything. To him, very politely, I retorted that he might do that on his own and spare his valued customer the bother. To which he giggled like a fool, and said if he did that he'd lose a good deal on commissions.

So I now asked for a rerating, and within a week had no blacksmith shop and no risk. I paid a fairly fair revised fee, and began to nurture my abiding and severe dislike of insurance "bahstards."

Next, mostly but not entirely for fun, I wrote to Elmo Scott Watson, who was the professor of journalism at Northwestern University and moonlit as editor of the *Publisher's Auxiliary*, the weekly newspaper of the Western Newspaper Union. I asked him to inquire if any newspaper in the United States had any record that a blacksmith shop ever burned down.

He did, and no such thing could be found.

There was no statistical proof whatever that a blacksmith shop was a hazard, a risk, to its combustible neighbors. The whole thing was a swindle, a profitable snack for the greedy insurance people.

Seven years later I got word that at long last a blacksmith shop had burned down. It is the only one on record. It was in Elmira, New York, and hadn't had a fire in its forge for forty-two smokeless years. It had been struck by lightning. Response by city firemen was immediate, and the small blaze had caused no damage to neighboring structures.

Back in our new apartment at Rhapsody Home, I thought about how I was being badgered because our old house was now on the market and unoccupied. I thought about that blacksmith shop and how it lingered in fancy to enrich the insurance folks. After thinking long enough and working up my grievance enough, I changed my residence to a seasonal dwelling, and my troubles are over. But I find Rhapsody Home continues to pay big-risk insurance premiums without a squawk and without a glance at imaginary risks, and then passes everything along on the rent bills. In the background, you can hear the mirthful hilarity of the insurance industry.

Not All Beans
Are Made the Same

The irresistible tendency to return frequently to food when writing about Rhapsody Home, or any happy retirement home, is understandable. Good food is what's craved most by us hopeful old timers, and if we don't get it, at least we can talk about it. I think the topic trumps even medical conditions for entertainment value.

The Down East baked bean, known in the Maine economy as the *logging berry,* has always been entertaining. An early recollection is of repeating the bean litany when one of us boys would let a fart go in the schoolyard, and everybody would singsong: Beans! Beans! The musical fruit. The more you eat, the more you toot.

The bean has something like twenty-three percent protein, and the rest is explosive. True, we good little boys and proper little girls did not let a brisk one fly as a social grace; we knew better. But as a testimonial of our general prowess, we'd give a good one publicity. The best fun was to flaunt one that would be hard to beat, and then judge the responses as offered. It has been said that early separatists chose the baked bean for weekend nourishment, as it relieved the household of cooking over the Sabbath. A pot of beans was ready to eat by Saturday supper, and beans were warmed for Sunday eating.

This brought Sunday devotions into the target area, and some of our best farts were heard or suppressed in church. Many's the demure maiden lady who thought she had a silent kind and came out loud and strong. It was pleasant to see her sitting there in the pew looking like the Twenty-Third Psalm and wondering if she'd soiled her drawers. Many, also, were they who refrained from offending at great risk, and then let go during the doxology, which was tumultuous enough to drown out all competition. Nobody heard these offerings, but there were lingering testimonials of what happened.

The baked bean has been so dominant in my fetching up and my growing old that I was properly glad to find it had come with me to Rhapsody Home, and would still be my Saturday night friend. On my first Saturday night, I arrived in the dining room to find baked beans and brown bread offered, and memories flooded upon me. Strange and uneasy, I was in a new situation to which I must adjust, yet here to welcome me was as old a friend as I have, a friend whose praises I had noised thousands of times, privately and publicly, and a friend I could trust always.

The bean seems to have been known and eaten from earliest days, but I wonder if its cultivation and use as we know it didn't develop in New England, and not necessarily in Boston, as an answer to the particular needs that came from our colonial living and our regional oddities. The bean produced well, and it stored easily and kept well. It was high in protein, and thus ideal for people doing heavy manual labor. On the farm and consequently in the woods, it was just the thing.

Felix Fernald, veteran woods clerk at the Great Northern Paper Company, used to tell of his first day at work. Breakfast at camp, then a walk before daylight to the sorting boom at Quakish Lake. At 9:30, the second breakfast came in pails, one of beans and one of biscuits. Then food arrived at intervals, beans and biscuits, until sundown, when the boys walked back to camp and had supper. Beans and biscuits can be eaten meal after meal, but some foods are resisted by the human stomach after a few repetitions. So baked beans became known as logging berries, and the Maine timberlands were harvested.

In the 1930s and 1940s came an effort by the CIO to organize the Maine woodsmen. There were difficulties. The gangsters sent up to do this knew nothing about the woods and had no idea what a chopper did. Many of the choppers were French-Canadians come down into Maine for employment, but the organizers didn't speak French. They did, however, use the baked bean as a reason for forming a union. It was un-American to feed so many baked beans. The timberland owners, very sensitive on the food line, took no chances. If the men were unhappy about food, a remedy must be found at once. Poor food causes fewer trees down. Baked beans were withdrawn from the camp menus, and this didn't matter because times had changed. Roads had been built and camps were no longer isolated by winter snow. Refrigeration had come along, and the keeping quality of dry beans was no longer important. It was curious to re-elect that lumber camps no longer served logging berries, but it was so.

But beans are always funny, and what do you suppose? Before long somebody said, "Why don't we get doze feves no more?" The men liked baked beans! They went back on lumber camp supply lists.

* * *

Maine's most gracious lady, the late Senator Margaret Chase Smith of Skowhegan, loved baked beans, too. In fact, they helped cement our friendship, which lasted until the end of her life. She told me, "The first time I accepted an invitation to speak to a Grange, I thought I'd get a good feed on down-to-earth baked beans, something I don't bake at home just for myself, and I didn't. I got a lovely turkey supper. Then I got more turkey suppers. All I ever get is a turkey supper. They think ordinary baked beans are a second-rate dish and they've got to have something better for the special guest. I haven't had a baked bean in months!"

I told Mrs. Smith that my best cook, thus far, baked a pot of Jacob's Cattle beans every Saturday, and our back door had no lock on it. She was welcome at any time. She said she would keep that in mind.

From then until Mrs. Smith became home-limited at her place in Skowhegan, she joined us now and then for Saturday night home-baked beans, with new bread and apple pie. These visits depended only on her having some kind of a political meeting in our neighborhood. If we had other guests, she'd come right in just the same. She'd lap up a plate of beans with piccalilli and weenie, or a slice of ham, as if baked beans were going out of style and she was eager to do what she could. Our two children knew discretion was polite, but were old enough to wonder what Mrs. Smith sounded like after our beans when she got back to Skowhegan. We never had a firsthand report.

Here at Rhapsody Home, as I have said, we do have the weekly offer of Saturday night beans, but after three tries I didn't try again. These institutional cooks open a can of baked beans, bring it out of lethargy into a warm persuasion, and send a serving to table with a reluctant hot dog and a slice of cold, canned brown bread. The plate has neither style nor flavor.

You can't serve beans straight from the can, and I know this on good authority. Have you heard of B & M beans? George Burnham Morrill inherited this family business of Burnham & Morrill Company, packers of quality baked beans, and subsequently sold it. But B & M products are still on the market. George thus had a good many million dollars in hand and had nothing to do except amuse himself. From time to time I would assist him. One day he said, "Our beans are not ready to eat. They come close, but there's no such thing as one flavor for all the millions that buy our beans. What you have to do is open the can and doctor the things. We have to assume that every good housewife knows how to do that. Little or a lot, depending on the family, fix 'em to taste."

Rhapsody Home has not learned to do that, yet. They need a better weenie, to start, and a warm slice of brown bread, perhaps with raisins. Their beans need some molasses, maple syrup, or brown sugar, just a bit, and a smidgen of dry mustard. I'd give 'em a bit of baking soda to lessen the gust, and always a pinch of ginger. It's up to you, but it needs doing. You've got to fetch the canned beans up to the perfection attained by those from a real bean pot in a kitchen where love prevails. So while baked beans are here at Rhapsody Home every Saturday night, they are not here. I pass them by and look the other way.

The Window Saga
Part III:
What's That Noise?

You'll recall how when we complained we could not open our bedroom window at night for ventilation, management kindly gave us a fan, because nothing could be done about the window! Despite the fan, our lack of fresh air continued to hinder our sleep. One day I asked if I might borrow an ax and a broom. I said I planned to smash out the window and then sweep up the glass. Then I said that next payday I would deduct something from my rent. That made them sit up, and they sent a young man to "see what he could do."

I showed him what he could do and how to do it, and the next day he took out the window and put hinges on it. Then he brought a long pole with a hook on it with which we could reach over the bed and behind the curtain, and by hunting around could find the latch and pull. This was wonderful and proved that something could be done after all. It would take us maybe a half-hour to move the bed, the desk, a chair, and a bookcase to get there with the pole, but we were willing to try.

It was a month or so after the window was fixed that we were awakened in the deep of the night by a whistle such as the Twentieth Century Limited used to blow when it went through Elkhart, Indiana. There is no railroad and no steamboat landing anywhere near Rhapsody Home.

"What was that?" my wife asked.

I arose from the prayer I had just uttered on my shaking knees, gave the question much thought, and said I did not know.

"It was under the bed!" she said.

In the next hour or so the whistle was blown several times. It could have been a fire alarm. It was like an extended cornet blast, as blown for yoicks at an English foxhunt. Or maybe a Greek tanker had sailed into our bathroom. We couldn't imagine what it was, whence it came, and why. After six or seven toots we gave up, and I telephoned the front desk of Rhapsody Home, where the night watchman said hello and we said, "What's the whistle?"

"What whistle?"

He promised to give this whistle immediate attention, and shortly a lady appeared to ask if she might be of assistance.

It was the window.

We now discovered that if we left our new and improved window open at the exact point where we wanted it at night, it became an incipient whistle and when the wind shifted south-southeast and breezed up, the aperture began to toot. All night. I found that by manipulating the window, I could play a tune!

Now we had a decision to make. Did we want the fresh air or a little quiet at night? As these are the kinds of questions old geezers in Rhapsody Homes have to answer, you might do well to think on this. From my personal experience I offer the following advice: If your windows begin to honk, enjoy it. It's the only way.

Grandfather Falls

My grandfather kept bees, and if he didn't have a comb of honey in the house when I came to visit, we'd go to open a hive and get some, assuming some was ready. Grandfather talked to his bees and told them everything that was going on, but he'd laugh about that and explain that bees had no ears and couldn't hear a word he said. But it was old folks' superstition that you should talk to your bees, and most important of all, tell them of a death in the family.

Grandfather had no fear of his bees and neither did I. Once in a while he'd get stung, and so would I. Grandfather said he'd been stung so much over the years that the venom no longer had any effect on him, but I would swell a bit from a sting, and he would put some baking soda on the place after he made sure the stinger was removed from my skin. He explained to me that a honeybee's stinger is a hypodermic needle and the venom sac comes away with the bee's stinger when it is left in my flesh. The natural tendency is to grasp at the stinger and pull it loose. This way the venom sac gets squeezed and you give yourself a sub-cutaneous injection, which makes things a good deal worse. To remove a stinger, he showed me, slide a knife blade under the sac and out comes the stinger with no squeeze.

Grandfather was forever carrying a box of honey to somebody as a gift. He sold his honey for twenty-five cents a pound, but the stores got it for fifteen cents and retailed it for the quarter. When I came to visit, I could have all the honey I wanted, and we kept pace, each to each. My grandfather lived alone by my time and cooked for himself, and he could make a pan of cream-tartar biscuits you wouldn't believe. Many's the time we'd make a meal of hot biscuits and honey.

Grampie told me the best honey our Maine bees make is from the apple bloom. Bees don't mix nectar, he said. Next to apple blossom, he liked the white clover. (Bees can't work red clover; their snouts aren't long enough to get into the blossoms.) Raspberry honey was nice, but after that the nectars started getting dark. Buckwheat honey was dark honey, and so was that of goldenrod and the late asters. The bass-wood trees were always in bloom, he said, by

July 21, and he liked buckwheat and basswood honey. So I listened, and so I "helped" Grampie, and I learned this and that and we both had a fine time.

I never went with him to Topsham Fair because of school, but he went every year and sold honey from a booth. He'd break open a pound-size comb and offer samples to folks passing that way, giving them tongue depressors instead of spoons. After a taste, most folks bought a box for a quarter. For quite a few years, he would take a working hive of bees to the fair, with a screen tent to contain the bees, and he'd give a talk off and on about bees. It was an attention getter, but involved more work than he thought it was worth. He found he sold about the same amount of honey whether he took the hive to fair or not.

But what I've been coming at is the time his bees almost killed him and what he said. It had to do with his Fameuse apple trees. The Fameuse, pronounced fay-muse by the folks back along, was also known as the Snow Apple, and it came in early fall. The apple wasn't a keeper, so it didn't go into the cellars for winter. It was good to eat when it began dropping from the tree. Grampie's three Fameuse trees were near the road, and easily subject to piracy. So he made a practice of taking a hive of bees over to be set near the Fameuse trees to discourage little boys and bigger boys from trespassing. It worked, and when it was time, Grandfather would tell his bees he was about to pick his apples and would come with a ladder and baskets to do so. His bees, naturally, kept flying and paid no attention, which they would also have done for thieves, but the thieves didn't know that. When the apples were gathered for the season, Gramp would take the beehives back to their stands.

So on this occasion, Grandfather was gathering his apples when a limb bent and he fell off his ladder. I forgot to say that this was in the fall of the year when he had his eighty-fourth birthday in April. Eighty years of age plus four for good measure is a nice age for picking apples off a ladder. Grandfather came down readily and hit the beehive with his back and broke three ribs.

He was strapped at the hospital, sent home, and cautioned to take it easy and avoid straining. When my father heard of this he hurried to the farm to see what he might do, and I went with him. We found Grandfather was doing, as the expression runs, as well as could be expected. He was glad to see us. He said, "It hurt! Godfrey Mighty, but it hurt! Why, it's had me hobblin' around here like an old man!"

So a man is as old as he feels, and that's a good thing to remember.

Testing

Doctors

Since the days of Hippocrates, it has been well known that nature cures the disease, and the treatment amuses the patient. But since the development of tests, the patient and nature bide, and the treatment amuses the physician. Here at our Rhapsody Home the doctor sits and looks at us and makes out a list of the tests he wants us to take. If we need more tincture of rhubarb to quiet our galloping diaphragms, there's a test to find out. After three intensive years of reading the results of tests, the medical student now gets three weeks of applied healing, and is ready to practice. So it seems.

Long before I was old enough to enjoy the miseries of advanced age tests, I watched a diphtheria epidemic. It started innocently enough. Dr. Woodrow, I believe it was, gave an ailing patient some pink pills (the blue pills were for broken bones) and things got better quickly. But the physical exercise teacher at the high school thought ahead of her time and said Dr. Woodrow ought to send swabs to the state laboratory for examination, and in a desire to please the woman he did just that. He was tremendously surprised when the report came back that the patient was suffering from diphtheria, and, as Dr. Woodrow had never seen diphtheria, he was sorry that his pink pills had already cured the patient.

To be on the safe side, he took swabs of the rest of the family, thirteen in number, and sent them to the state laboratory. To his dismay, reports came back that they all had diphtheria, even though at the moment they all seemed in good health. Dr. Woodrow went to the drugstore, where they had a telephone, and called the state laboratory to talk to Dr. Coombs, who was the State Director of Public Health, and asked him what he should do. Dr. Coombs suggested quarantine, and Dr. Woodrow began putting little yellow tags on doorknobs. In this way the epidemic spread and hysteria bloomed, and the town had to get more little yellow cards printed at the Doyle & Stover print shop. Shortly, nearly every house in town had a yellow card and schools were closed. Christmas was in two weeks, and storekeepers complained.

About now another physician in town, Dr. Richardson, older and better filled with wisdom, who had played no part in the diphtheria scare, decided to involve himself, and he went to the drugstore and called his friend at Boston City Hospital, an M.D. named Plaice, the head of the contagion ward. Dr. Plaice came to town at once, and a little gathering of doctors and nurses was arranged to hear his remarks.

He said, simply enough, that diphtheria evidence is always present but suppressed, and it offers no threat unless it becomes virulent, whereupon in serious cases surgery may be needed to allow bypass breathing. He told everybody present, but Dr. Woodrow in particular, that if diphtheria was showing on state lab tests, it would be well, before taking drastic steps, to send each report back and ask for a virulency test. This, he said, was a bit harder to do, and he suspected that the state lab would immediately cease to find quite so much diphtheria. And that is what happened. When good Dr. Coombs cried, "Diphtheria!" good Dr. Woodrow replied, "Virulency?" and Dr. Coombs permitted everything to subside.

When I had achieved a certain age, I started making regular trips to a physician for what my friend Marcel Laverdiere called "periodic checkups from time to time." David Bradeen was a young man we came to know when he was getting his medical degree, and we signed up right after he received it to give him something to do until he built up his practice. By that time Medicare was ready to start paying us, and we felt we should cooperate. Dr. David was great on tests, and before I was much older I had all of them save the mammogram. One of the tests was an exploration of my colon, and Dr. David said that he could send me to a specialist for it, but he had never done one and would like to try it. I asssented, and on a given morning we met at the hospital lab to look into matters.

It really wasn't a bad experience. Dr. David looked into my colon and was much impressed. He said he had enjoyed every minute. He said it was great fun, and reminded him ever-so-much of his honeymoon experience in a glass-bottomed boat through the Blue Grotto. He said I was beautiful, and he would keep the pictures by his bedside constantly. He paid me thirty dollars.

There was one test that I refused to take because I had to lie flat on a steel board and I just couldn't do it. They admitted it was something few people had ever been able to do. A month or so later they had a new way to pose that picture by having the patient sit in a rocking chair, and in this way medical inspections have made great strides.

I guess I have been lucky in my dealings

with the medical profession. When I was a kid, I had measles, chicken pox, mumps, and whooping cough. I think I may have had Spanish influenza in 1918, but am not sure, and neither was the doctor. Most people who developed the Spanish influenza went quietly, and the medical folks treated it like pneumonia, or more often something they could spell, and funerals were staggered. I do remember occasional lucid moments when the ceiling over my bed stopped going one way and reversed. My mother said I was terribly sick. I knew of no reason to dispute her. But nobody ever came right out to say I had the flu, and perhaps I didn't.

I did break two arms. The first time it was my right arm, and consisted of a clean fracture that hurt like the devil. I was eight years old and I fell through the hole where hay was shoved down to a long-ago horse. There had been no hay there to fall on for about eighty years, and my descent amounted to ten feet. The fracture was reduced by a Dr. Gahagan, pronounced Gan, who was a red-headed Irishman who probably studied medicine in a brickyard. He said, "This is going to hurt," and then he pulled my hand with one of his and pulled my arm with the other. I've never forgotten how that hurt.

Six years later I fell off a hayrack while

building load for Joe Veno, and landed on my own left hand. Joe said, "I hear doze t'ing crack!" So did I. It was a Corliss's fracture, in which all the bones of the forearm, wrist, and fingers as far back as 1776 became socially involved. Dr. Arthur L. Gould, no relation, of Freeport looked at my arm, said, "I love to set bones!" and set them. I did get ether that time. Dr. Gould had yet to know about an X-ray test. I surmise he might have refused to use it on the grounds it was new and undependable. But maybe not, he did have the first snowmobile in the state.

Now, at Rhapsody Home, I think of Dr. Gould and Dr. Woodrow and Dr. Coombs and Dr. Richardson and Dr. Plaice and Dr. Gahagan, and I go for my tests and find them amusing. So far, anyway.

What You Have to Do Is . . .

Long years ago now, before we even thought about getting involved with Rhapsody Home, my wife was looking at a catalog, and she interrupted my consideration of the Aristotelian quandaries by saying, "Do we have a coat of arms?"

I said we certainly did, it was a keg of cider, rampant on a field of buckwheat, why?

She said they had a wine goblet at JC Penney with our coat of arms on it. "So we do have one," I said.

Then she said, "I wonder what it looks like."

I said, "Why don't you buy a wine goblet and find out? I can use a wine goblet for collar buttons and cuff links."

So that's how that came about, and that's what she did. I had no reason to be apprehensive about Mr. Penney, but to be sure I inspected the order when I wrote the check, and it was all right. She ordered one wine goblet with our family coat of arms, and payment was inclusive of postage and handling. I was curious myself about our family coat of arms. Why the hell would we have any? Was some ancient ancestor a Knight of the Table Round?

Mr. Penney was prompt. Nicely wrapped and clearly marked *fragile,* the package was in our contract route box and we got a look at our family coat of arms. It didn't convince me, really, as I still think our family coat of arms should properly be something more like two manure forks sticking out under a barn, but I think my dear wife was impressed for she called me Sir Galahad for a day or so.

In the next step, my life was changed completely, and I found I was no longer idle in a contented world of common sense, but was a victim of the computer in its mad prance of idiocy. My wife set the wine goblet on the shelf, an odd piece to go with a moustache cup, some salt dishes, a bonbon saucer, and so on, and we picked up our lives again and sauntered on. Then, in one month, we got a package from JCPenney, and we had our second wine goblet with our family coat of arms and a bill, for which Mr. Penney would accept any major credit card. (I hope Major Credit Card someday gets on the Pentagon staff.) If you have been reading my published material, you already know that, since my Youth's

Companion days, I have been solidly opposed to foolishment, so I tossed Mr. Penney's bill in the pail, put the second goblet on the shelf, and went down to find a mess of clams. One month later we got a third goblet.

When we had sixteen goblets, and Mr. Penney was nasty about our financial cooperation, I happened to pass (I did not make a special trip) Mr. Penney's big store, and I inquired in congenial fashion for the manager. He was pleasant enough, and said that I must have ordered a goblet a month, or I wouldn't be getting them. I said I had not, and that as the goblets arrived monthly they were set upon the shelf in our home, and would be awaiting him there when he decided to come and get them. I said I would not expect the shelf to collapse for another year or so. Then, the manager of the JCPenney store said the magic words that opened the gate and permitted me to enter the new computerized world.

He said, "Now, what you have to do is . . ."

Me? Why do I have to do anything?

The reason we are in a computerized world is the ridiculous willingness of innocent and victimized people to go ahead and do what the computerized program tells them to do. The manager said I had to go to the post office and fill out a form.

I do not know if Mr. Penney got his goblets

back. The last I know we had the first one on our shelf, and 159 others in boxes in the back end of the woodshed. I told the manager he could come and get them anytime. I was told shortly thereafter that the JCPenney store had terminated its great service to the people of Maine, but would continue mailing wine goblets and other items as ordered.

So that was my introduction to the new method of big business, and since then I have been told hundreds of times, "Now, what you have to do is . . . "

And hundreds of times I have taken a deep breath, counted to ten, and responded (as everybody should) in this polite and effective manner: "What you need to do is defecate in your chapeau."

I will give the details on one incident of this sort that is still to be settled at Rhapsody Home, where we are so pleasantly shielded against anything of the sort. It has to do with my wife's bath. At the moment, her bath is computed at fifteen dollars the dunk, but the management is defecating in the corporate chapeau, and I think in the end we may get a better arrangement.

Before we arrived at Rhapsody Home, we revealed our total situation. We made our assets public and signed away our all. We explained our physical conditions, and in particular for this narrative, we gave every detail of my wife's hip and knee surgery, which understandably prevents her cavorting on maypole day and again for the trick-or-treat on Halloween. All this, plus everything else, went into the computer to govern our remaining days. Specifically, this included our Medicare and insurance status, up and down the mast. You bet.

And, when we moved in to commence our total enjoyment of the pleasures and benefits arranged, we found that our bathtub was of such a style and was so located that my darling wife could not frame to approach it right and faced a dirty future. She tried, we tried, and it was no go. When we expostulated to management, we were told we had their complete sympathy, but that nothing could be done about it and it would be done immediately.

Nothing, really, was done about it, but a young lady began to appear on stated days, and she would bathe my wife luxuriously. Being professionally trained, this young lady knew how to get my wife's abused limbs adjusted and in just about seven minutes would hang up the wet towel, bid me to have a good day, and be gone.

Then, each month, the Rhapsody House computer put fifteen dollars for each bath on our bill.

Considering everything, mainly that my wife might soap herself down if the architect had been bright, I mentioned using the hat, and things rest there, I suppose. The bath, when it occurs, is billed under "HHA." They told me this stands for Home Health Aid, and what I had to do was get in touch with Medicare B, and they would tell me what to do next. As I said to that JCPenney manager some years ago, "Me? Why do I have to do anything?" We're at a standoff now. I mention this now only to arm future Rhapsody Home residents with the knowledge that they may end up living in the equivalent of a JCPenney store.

Staff of Life

Now we have arrived at the subject of our daily bread. If, like me, you have lived a good life of good loaves, you will find moving into a senior slot is much more than an occasion for prayer. From earliest boyhood I have regularly and without fail besought our Heavenly Father to fetch me my daily bread, and He has done so to keep me nourished, grateful, and satisfied. But when I became old and moved into Rhapsody Home to squander my assets in gracious if riotous living, He has forsaken me and I get something else, which I'm sure any nutritionist will tell me is just as good. Maybe even better.

To mitigate some of the idle vituperation I am going to lavish on this matter, I will first tell the story of Mr. Thadeus Goodspeed of New York City. This will show how important bread can be, and to say that I am well aware that some people hanker for bread more than do some others.

* * *

Mr. Goodspeed liked bread. Mr. Goodspeed was also the one for dining out, and when told of a good place that was new to him, he went to it at once. So he came to the restaurant Chez Charles in the Village one evening and was greeted with Gallic fervor and shown to a seat, where he found the menu exciting. Everything pleased him. The waiters were incredible. His every wish was anticipated. The food was beyond compare, the music was just right. Before leaving he told all this to the head waiter and added, "My only criticism is that I got only two slices of bread."

The waiter said, "You like bread?"

"Yes, indeed! The bread was fine, but I got only two slices!"

"When you come again, sir, we shall remember that!"

And when Mr. Goodspeed came again he was remembered, and he got four slices of bread.

However, upon expressing his disappointment that the amount of bread served was not up to his expectations, the waiter again promised to do better next time. And each time Mr. Goodspeed came he got more bread. Next time it was six slices, and eight slices, and ten slices, and then twelve slices. Each time he gave the food and ambience his utter approval, but said there wasn't enough bread.

The next time Mr. Goodspeed came, for Chez Charles was now his favorite, except for bread, the chef saw him being seated and said, "This time I'll fix the bastard." And he took a long loaf of fat French bread, and he sliced it down the middle of its ample three feet, and then gave it a sufficiency of a special garlic butter for which Chez Charles was famous. He laid it on a great platter, garnished it with a sprig of parsley, and said, "Stick that under his nose and see what he says!"

Again, Mr. Goodspeed greatly relished his supper. When the head waiter asked him if he had enjoyed his meal, Mr. Goodspeed made reply as follows: "Everything was superb. I believe this was the finest dinner I have enjoyed in my entire life! But tell me, why did you go back to just two slices of bread?"

I was about to write that my mother never bought a loaf of store bread, but that is not true. Every so often she would give me six cents and tell me to run down to the Dillingham store and get a loaf of stale bread. In those days the bread foundries had not taken over entirely, but Mr. Dillingham did sell some store bread, even if he still handled flour by the barrel. A loaf of fresh bread sold for seven cents. For six I could get yesterday's. I'd look up at Mr. Dillingham and Mr. Dillingham would look down at me, and I'd pass him my six cents and ask for a loaf of stale bread. He'd pat my head and grin, and say, "Time to roast another rooster, eh, Johnny?" My mother always had fresh bread in her crockery bread jar, but the best poultry stufflng is made from older stuff. The rooster was a volunteer from our own flock.

My mother baked two double loaves of bread every Wednesday and Saturday. Those on Saturday shared the heat of the Modern Clarion wood-burning kitchen range with pies and cakes and sundries and the weekly pot of baked beans. I remember that, during the war, a general in resplendent medals came to my primary school to give us a recipe for a bread approved by the government, which would save money and help win the war. I took the recipe home to Mom, and she said it would cost thirty cents a loaf more than the bread she was already making and what was the matter with the schools, anyway? She told me, "When there's something better, Mummy will make it!" My wife never bought bread, either.

Plain bread is not the only bread that has made me glad. Here at Rhapsody Home I'd like to see some of my old bread friends again—like the deacon's blueberry cake. This was not a cake. It was a hot bread served with the meat, baked in a big cake pan or on a baker's sheet and cut into pieces about three inches square. Slather it with butter, and it goes good with anything, like an ear of sweet corn. In Maine, all references to blueberries mean wild blueberries, preferably caught in their native lair that morning with the dew still showing. You can make this cake with cultivated New Jersey Blues and get away with it, and you can also make it with Maine blueberries that have been frozen since last July. Don't quibble, just make it.

Something else we loved, as a variation on plain bread, was the joyful St. John the Baptist. In Maine's St. John River Valley, where this delicacy originated, the folks call it by a very indecent term, so uncouth that an experienced dog, asleep under the stove, upon hearing it, will wake, excuse himself, and want out, but as St. John the Baptist it gains respect and may be enjoyed by the most fastidious. It is made from bread dough cut off during its first rising and shaped into a patty that is fried in salt pork or bacon fat until crisp on both sides and amorous in the middle. Eat with jelly or jam, or with warm maple syrup. Because of its origin among the Valley Acadians, do not confuse it with plogues, which are not bread but are pancakes of buckwheat flour served with wild strawberry jam instead of maple syrup. It would be nice if Rhapsody Home would serve St. John the Baptists or plogues, but it does not.

And yeast rolls. These were merely bread dough raised to the third power and then baked off as biscuits. Dip each darling in butter so they'll come apart later, and bake in a cake pan. And stand back, for the cheers can deafen.

We'd just about given up on a getting a good loaf of bread when our friend Joe Novick came to call, and hope lifted its doubtful head and we felt better. Joe began bringing us loaves of bread at unscheduled times, and we could take a slice or two down to the dining room every evening and tell folks God was again on duty. Joe had a bread-making machine and he loved to use it. Joe took over where the Almighty took off. Fact is, Joe liked his machine so well he left it at camp up in the woods and bought a second one to use at home downstate. I thought it might be possible that the cook would see us come in bearing nice bread and take umbrage, possibly cutting our throats in rage, but he seems not to notice, perhaps too busy mixing his green peas with his goddam carrots.

As winter drew on, we felt Joe's driving over to our Happy Haven might sometimes be treacherous, so we bought a bread machine and began to make our own. It is great. We now mix a batch, heave it into the thing, and then polish our nails until the bread is ready to go downstairs and give us support while we eat. To those of you good people who have lived contentedly with home-baked bread and are now aged and hungry and thinking about a pleasant retirement home, I implore you to pay attention in particular to the matter of bread. Our Father Which Art in Heaven just isn't going to come every morning bearing a loaf of His sweet fresh bread.

And now I leave you with a riddle: Why is a loaf of bread like the sun? Because it rises in the yeast and sets behind the vest!

Dining Out

All young people, looking forward to old age when they can enroll in a Rhapsody Home, will want to give thought to an evening on the town, with dinner at some delightful Wayside Inn. The sheltered life at a Rhapsody Home has its advantages, but it will be pleasant to get away now and then. A son or a daughter, no doubt, and grandchildren, too, will help. For such happy interludes, the restaurant must be chosen with care. Of course, an establishment with good bread is important, but they should also hold the door open while you go in, and again while you go out, and when you leave they must hand you your doggie bag. Our children arranged a night out recently, and it was a total success.

First, we telephoned down to the Rhapsody Home dining room and told them we would be obliged this evening to forego the lovely meat loaf with macaroni and cheese, as we were being taken to dinner by our children. When the time came we sat outside our apartment door to watch our fellow residents go to supper, and we wished them jolly good appetites without being overly obnoxious. We realized we were envied just as we had envied others on their nights out, but we would be back the next evening to rejoin the pleasures of senior living.

Our daughter was punctual. We were meeting our son and suite at the restaurant.

At Rhapsody Home we come to supper as John and Dorothy, and we have the choice of potato cream soup. Now, supported solicitously by son and daughter, aluminum walkers in step, the door is opened for us by a smiling good-looker who never saw us before and doesn't know feet-up from a Vasotec-20 pill, but arranges our chairs anyway. All at once I realized I was real people again, not an institutionalized social security number relegated to residual indifference. And it is inspiring to be recognized as halfway cripples, out for a toot, rather than just one of the bunch. At Rhapsody Home it's no great shakes to be old. But this evening I thought I could hear the other patrons: "Oh, just look at that poor old gaffer! See how he trips on the carpet! Such a fine looking man, and so young for his age! Thank heaven he sat down before he fell!"

Something particularly noticeable is the difference in conversations at Rhapsody Home and at a restaurant night out. At Rhapsody Home, as I have mentioned, colloquy runs largely to ailments and their cures and the handy adjacency of a pharmacy that will charge and deliver. But when unleashed, Rhapsody Home residents like us reveal great interest in many other phases of human affairs, and this is good. All during supper, at our Wayside Inn, we talked about the state of the union, about travels, about sports and work and hobbies, about our grandchildren's school and friends, and more. Families provide sunshine in a residual area of shade.

When our waitress came to ask if things were all right, I looked at our son and I looked at our daughter, and I said, "Yes."

Old Friends

When you have made the big decision and all is arranged and you have moved into your new digs, you find with a deep-seated pang that none of your old friends has joined you. And while it's true that I am making new friends amongst the jolly inmates, old friends and friends who are old are different friends.

I've noticed a severe change in the grocery club. Before we came to Rhapsody Home, we went on our own every Tuesday morning to shop, and we—the menfolk of our town— would hold our little meeting by the rest benches while the ladyfolk spent the money. Everybody knew us and everybody spoke. The manager, who was an Acadian from the Valley, joined us, and sometimes we would fire him and sometimes we'd raise his pay. We all loved a gracious lady who wore a coonskin hat, but we never knew who she was. We had fun because we made fun, and folks we had never seen before would sidle in to find out what was so funny, and we'd elect them to life membership and give them a twenty percent discount on their groceries. There was a memorable Tuesday when we got everybody in the store singing "Three Blind Mice."

You'll find communities and circumstances differ. Here at Rhapsody Home, they fetch out the corporate bus once a week, and everybody goes to buy groceries. We parade into the store with the fierce aggression of a Scottish curling club on its way to a bonspiel, and the clerks modestly turn their heads aside and eye us askance, as if we mustn't be trusted. Being aged and infirm and accustomed to friendly attention, I asked in the new store where they hid the paper clips, and a young lady pointed. They were right beside a sign that said, *we are here to serve you.*

It's not all bad; it's just different. I sit on a bench, much like the old one, and the store manager speaks to me, and he is pleasant and jovial. But a character he ain't, or if he is he doesn't want to let go and be noticed. It takes all kinds, and as Peter Partout used to say, he was glad he warn't one of 'em. Too few people, I believe, get to be proficient nuts. I don't mean, at all, the clinical nut who has something the matter with him, but the pro-

fessional nut, like Bill Zorack, who could re-
cite Spartacus to the Gladiators in Yiddish. Or
Bert Coombs, piano tuner, real estate dealer,
tinsel manufacturer, violin maker, and blacksmith, just to name a few of his vocations.
And Gerald Spide, who served elegant dinners
on the finest china, then refused to wash the
dishes because it was easier to wipe them with
a paper towel. Lumberjack Del Bates had a
story for every occasion. Guy Rogers may not
have been the smartest chap, but he was still
the best ice harvester in Maine. All of these
dear friends did things that many times I've
wished I might do, or had done. I miss the old
gang. I keep them in mind. They sustain me.

I did have one fine day at the Rhapsody
store. An old gentleman who looked about
half my age came out of the crowd to share
my waiting bench, and as he settled in I said,
"Think they'll have it?"
He said, "It was last week."
So I said, "Then I missed it."
He said, "It's possible."
And then he told me he slipped on the ice
in his barnyard, had to crawl hands and knees
until he found a purchase, and then stood up
to find he'd lost his teeth. He fummy-diddled
around, fell again, spent way too much time
looking, but couldn't find them. Then he re-

membered he hadn't put 'em in that morning and they were in a glass of water on the piano. He'd left them there while he played Sousa's "Seventy-six Trombones," which he did every morning at 7:15. Then he asked if anything like that had happened to me lately. If I find a few others like him, we may organize the Rhapsody Home Nuts yet.

Much Too Young?

Summing things up, as we should do about now, calls for a reference to *De Senectute,* in English, *Old Age,* the essay of Marcus Tullius Cicero written in 44 B.C. I, and numerous others, read it when we were young, perhaps in high school Latin class, in the blithe days when growing old wasn't important. The year I was fifty, I began making a practice of rereading *De Senectute* every October 22, my birthday and also my anniversary. Each year I find something in it I had not appreciated the previous year. I recommend reading it before moving to your own Rhapsody Home. It will tell you how to be young when you are very old.

A friend once made the sensible remark that there was no great trick to growing old. Anybody can do it by living long enough. My mother had a sister who lived to be 102, and then my mother lived to be 103. There has always been something of a contest about old age in my family. Perhaps in other families as well. I heard Linnie Prout and her cousin Ted Wallace discussing this one day at Merrill's Livery Stable.

Linnie said, "How old be ye, Ted?"

And Ted made answer by saying, "How old be ye?"

"No," said Linnie, "I asked you first."

"Well," said Ted, "I'll be eighty-eight come August nine."

"By the Lord Harry," said Linnie, "I got you beat!"

I was to learn that it is indeed an achievement to become eighty-eight, but by that time I was housed up in comprehensive desuetude and had nothing more to brag about.

Perhaps you have heard the story about the aging Highland Scot who answered the summons of the clan and took his son along to help him get around and to give the lad experience in the noble Scottish ways. There broke out one of those frequent skirmishes the Scots developed now and then to fret the English, and now the Highlanders were up in the hills about to bed down for the night, kilts a-tilt and snow a foot deep. The son, arranging things for the night, scooped together some loose snow and patted it into position to make himself a pillow for his slumbers. Thus cushioned, he arranged his plaid and closed his eyes. Now comes the father, and seeing his son in calm and easy sleep, he pushes away the wee pile of snow under the boy's neck, and in utter disgust he says, "Ye're much too young for comfort!"

I think on that story a lot as I absorb the care and attention provided here at Rhapsody Home. It is true that I am generally well off and I am lucky that my loving wife is here with me and that we are in such good company. Most of us seniors have bought and sold and mastered our trades. We have had our babies, seen them grow and give us grandchildren and great-grandchildren. We laid by some, gave to the Salvation Army, and kept the faith. We laughed and cried and shunned evil, and we always voted more pay for schoolteachers. Life was good to us, mostly, and we were in favor of it. Now the dust from our frantic efforts has subsided, our young ones are paying the taxes we rashly embraced, and the world has turned 'round.

Well, they've taken me out of the Maine woods and buttoned me up in the new wilderness of tranquil senility, but it may well be that I, at a mere ninety, am still much too young for the wonderful comforts of Rhapsody Home.